W9-CVO-330

THE OFFICIAL BUS HANDBOOK

This handbook is only a guide. For official purposes, please refer to the Ontario Highway Traffic Act and regulations as well as the Public Vehicles Act and Regulations.

For more information about driver licensing, visit www.mto.gov.on.ca.

To request a copy of this book in an alternate format, contact Publications Ontario at 1-800-668-9938 or (416) 326-5300 or visit www.publications.serviceontario.ca.

Disponible en français
Demandez le « Guide officiel des autobus »

Driving is a privilege — not a right

Introduction

This handbook is designed to help drivers who want to apply for licences to operate buses, school buses and ambulances: classes B, C, E or F driver's licences.

As well as the rules of the road, bus and ambulance drivers need to know the laws governing the operation of vehicles that transport passengers. They must have special driving skills and demonstrate the safe driving practices that apply to those vehicles.

This handbook sets out the information you will need to know and the skills you will be expected to demonstrate in order to qualify for these licences.

CONTENTS

Chapter 1

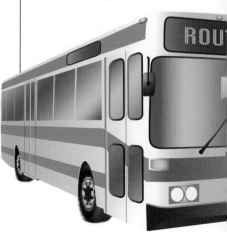

GETTING YOUR
LICENCE

I. Legislation

These Acts and Regulations govern certain aspects of the movement of passengers and goods, and the operation of vehicles.

1. The Highway Traffic Act (HTA) and regulations govern the driver, the vehicle and equipment, weight and numbers of passengers that a bus driver can carry.
2. The Motor Vehicle Transport Act (Federal) regulates the for hire transportation of goods and people.
3. The Public Vehicles Act and regulations control the for hire movement of people on the highways by bus.

II. Licence classes and combinations

The Driver's Licence Classification Chart on pages 8-9 shows you what class of licence you need to drive different vehicles.

A driver may hold a class A, B, C, D, E, F, G, G1, G2, M, M with L condition, M1, M2, or M2 with L condition driver's licence or combination. A full class G licence is required to apply for a Class A, B, C, D, E or F licence. A novice driver may not hold a classified licence or a driving instructor's licence.

There are several possible combinations of licences. For example, you can hold a class A and B if you meet the requirements for both. Your licence designation in this case would be shown as AB.

Any class or combination of licence classes from G to A may be combined with a class M licence authorizing the operation of motorcycles if you meet the requirements for class M. The combinations AM, EM, ABM and so on, are other examples of combinations.

7

Driver's Licence Classification Chart

Class of Licence	Types of vehicles allowed	May also drive vehicle in class
A	Any tractor-trailer combination	D and G
B	Any school purposes bus	C, D, E, F and G
C	Any regular bus	D, F and G
D	Any truck or combination provided the towed vehicle is not over 4,600 kg	G
E	School purposes bus – maximum of 24-passenger capacity	F and G
F	Regular bus – maximum of 24-passenger capacity – and ambulances	G

Diagram 1-1a

Driver's Licence Classification Chart

Class of Licence	Types of vehicles allowed	May also drive vehicle in class
G	Any car, van or small truck or combination of vehicle and towed vehicle up to 11,000 kg provided the towed vehicle is not over 4,600 kg	
G1	Level One of graduated licensing. Holders may drive Class G vehicles with an accompanying fully licensed driver with at least four years' driving experience. Subject to certain conditions.	
G2	Level Two of graduated licensing. Holders may drive Class G vehicles without accompanying driver but are subject to certain conditions.	
M	Motorcycles, including limited-speed motorcycles (motor scooters) and motor-assisted bicycles (mopeds). Holders may also drive a Class G vehicle under the conditions that apply to a Class G1 licence holder.	
M1	Level One of graduated licensing for motorcycles, including limited-speed motorcycles (motor scooters) and motor-assisted bicycles (mopeds). Holders may drive a motorcycle under certain conditions.	
M2	Level Two of graduated licensing for motorcycles, including limited-speed motorcycles (motor scooters) and motor-assisted bicycles (mopeds). Holders may drive a motorcycle but only with a zero blood alcohol level. Holders may also drive a Class G vehicle under the conditions that apply to a Class G1 licence holder.	
M with L condition	Holders may operate a limited-speed motorcycle or moped only	May operate a limited speed motorcycle or moped only
M2 with L condition	Holders may operate a limited-speed motorcycle or moped only	May operate a limited speed motorcycle or moped only

Diagram 1-1b

A "Z" air brake endorsement is required on a driver's licence to operate any air brake equipped motor vehicle.

Medical requirements for classified licences

When applying for a class A, B, C, D, E or F licence, you must provide a completed ministry medical certificate. You can get blank medical forms from any DriveTest Centre in Ontario. A licence will be refused if your physical or medical condition does not meet the standards outlined in the regulations of the Highway Traffic Act.

Drivers under the age of 46 must submit a medical report every **five** years. Drivers aged 46 to 64 must submit a medical report every **three** years. Drivers aged 65 and older are required to submit a medical report every year.

If your licence is conditional on wearing corrective lenses, do not drive without wearing them. Your medical practitioner or optometrist is required by law to report to the licensing authorities any health problems that might affect your safe operation of a motor vehicle.

Chapter 1, section II — Summary

By the end of this section you should know:
- The different licence classifications and what they permit you to drive
- The medical requirements you must meet to maintain a bus driver's licence

III. Bus Licence Classes C and F

A class C licence is needed to drive any bus with seats for more than twenty-four (24) passengers, but not a school purposes bus carrying passengers. It allows the driver to operate vehicles included in classes D, F and G, but not motorcycles.

A class F licence is needed to drive an ambulance or any bus with seats for ten (10) or more passengers, but not more than twenty-four (24) passengers, and not a school purposes bus carrying passengers. It also allows the driver to operate vehicles included in class G, but not motorcycles.

Definitions

Here are definitions of some words used in this section.
- **Highway:** a common and public highway, street, avenue, parkway, driveway, square, place, bridge, viaduct or trestle, any part of which is used by the public for

the passage of vehicles, including the shoulders of the road and the land between property lines.
- **Roadway:** the part of the highway that is designed or ordinarily used for traffic, not including the shoulder. Where a highway includes two or more separate roadways, the term roadway refers to any one roadway and not all of the roadways together.
- **Bus:** a motor vehicle designed and used for carrying ten or more passengers.

An applicant for a class C or F driver's licence must:
- be at least 18 years of age,
- hold a valid Ontario class G or higher licence or equivalent issued in a province or territory of Canada,
- meet medical and vision standards,
- have knowledge of bus equipment maintenance and passenger safety and control,

- pass an MTO driver examination or obtain a certificate of competence from a recognized authority by passing a vision screening, a knowledge test and a driving test in a vehicle of appropriate size.

How to obtain a class C or F driver's licence
1. Pick up the necessary forms from any DriveTest Centre in Ontario, including the medical examination report and study material.
2. Take the medical report to a physician of your choice. When the medical report has been completed, return it to the DriveTest Centre selected for your test. Only applicants with satisfactory medical reports may take a knowledge test for a classified licence.
3. You will be required to pass the following tests:
   - A vision screening
   - A knowledge test including traffic signs recognition and

operating knowledge of a bus or ambulance
- An on-road test in a vehicle with an appropriate number of seats
- A satisfactory driver record search

Vision and knowledge test checklist, classes C and F
Before taking the class C or F knowledge test, make sure you have studied the Official Bus Handbook.

Bring the following items to the test:
- 2 pieces of identification or Ontario Driver's Licence
- Complete medical report form
- Money for test fees — cash, debit or credit card
- Glasses or contact lenses (if you need to wear them to read or write)

Road test, classes C and F
During your road test —
- You will be asked to demonstrate

a daily trip inspection known as a circle check. You will name the item of equipment checked and briefly describe its condition.

- You will be required to drive in traffic and handle the vehicle safely according to the class of licence for which you are applying.
- You may be required to reverse the vehicle into a parking bay or marked area.

Road test checklist, classes C and F

Bring the following items to the road test:

- Appropriate vehicle in good working order
- Money for test fees (if applicable)
- Glasses (if you need to wear them to drive)
- Wheel chocks or blocks, if the vehicle is equipped with air brakes

Arrive at least 30 minutes before your road test appointment. All road tests have a set time frame. Before you begin your test, the examiner will inform you of the amount of time you have to complete it.

Daily trip inspection, classes C and F

Driver's circle check

A driver is not permitted to drive a bus; motor coach; school bus; or, a school purposes bus, van or station wagon unless the driver or another person has, within the previous 24 hours, conducted an inspection of the vehicle and completed an inspection report. The driver must continue to check all systems throughout the day because the condition of the vehicle can change. By staying alert, you can spot trouble before it causes a breakdown or collision.

The inspection is conducted in accordance with an inspection schedule. The schedule provides a list of vehicle systems and components that the driver is required to inspect and provides a list of defects to guide and assist the driver.

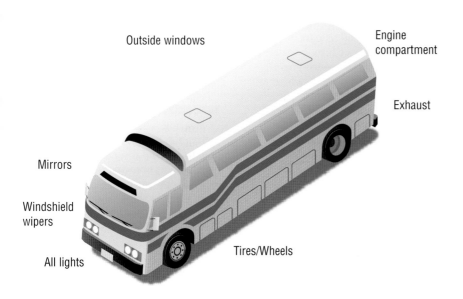

Mirrors

Windshield wipers

All lights

Outside windows

Engine compartment

Exhaust

Tires/Wheels

Diagram 1-1

The schedule used for the inspection depends upon the type of bus and its use as follows:

Schedule 2: buses, motor coaches, trailers towed by either vehicle

Schedule 5: yellow school buses, school-purposes buses

Schedule 6: school-purposes vans or station wagons when carrying six or more passengers

The inspection schedule divides defects into two categories, major and minor. When a minor defect is identified, the driver must record the defect on the inspection report and report the defect to the operator. Drivers are not permitted to drive a vehicle with a major defect.

Drivers must carry both the current inspection report and the applicable inspection schedule. Electronic reports and schedules are permitted.

Schedules 3 and 4 for motor coaches

Motor coach operators have a second inspection process available to them.

The requirements allow the operator to select either the regular bus inspection process using Schedule 2 as described above, which requires the driver to verify there are no under-vehicle defects, or inspect the bus using a two stage inspection process.

Under the two-stage process the driver conducts an inspection of the coach using Schedule 3. A Schedule 3 inspection is similar to a Schedule 2 inspection but omits the under-vehicle inspection requirements for the driver. The Schedule 3 inspection is also valid for 24 hours. As with a Schedule 2 inspection the driver is required to examine and observe the condition of the vehicle during the day or trip.

A Schedule 3 inspection is only valid when the coach has also had a Schedule 4 inspection. A Schedule 4 inspection is conducted by a coach technician and is valid for 30 days or 12,000 kms, whichever comes first. The Schedule 4 inspection consists of a detailed under-vehicle inspection.

The daily trip inspection or circle check in this book shows the absolute minimum inspection that must be performed as part of the driver testing procedure. For the full inspection schedules outlining all major and minor defects, which all commercial vehicle drivers are required to complete daily, refer to the Ontario Regulation 199/07 "Commercial Motor Vehicle Inspections" in the Highway Traffic Act at www.e-laws.gov.on.ca.

Outside inspection
- Headlights, turn signals, parking and clearance lights
- Windshield and wipers
- Engine compartment: fluid levels, wiring, belts, hoses and hydraulic brake fluid leaks (if so equipped)
- Tires
- Exposed wheel nuts, lugs and studs
- Exhaust system (check for leaks)
- Stop, tail and hazard lights
- Emergency exits
- Rear windows (check for cleanliness) if applicable
- Entrance door
- Body condition (check for sharp edges)
- Fuel system (tank, cap and check for leaks)

Inside inspection
- Steering wheel (for excessive freeplay)
- Brake pedal reserve and fade
- Brake booster operation
- Brake failure warning light
- Parking brake operation
- Brake air pressure or vacuum gauge
- Warning signal, low air pressure/vacuum gauge
- Turn indicator and hazard lights, switch and pilot
- Interior lights
- Windshield washer and wipers
- Windshield and windows

- Mirrors, adjustment and condition
- Defroster and heaters
- Horn
- Driver's seat belt and seat security
- Emergency equipment
- Emergency exits

Note: If the vehicle is being used as a school purposes vehicle, the daily trip inspection used will be the one on pages 20 to 23, for school purposes vehicles.

The daily road check (while driving the vehicle)

Drivers are required to examine and observe the condition of the vehicle during the day or trip. Plan a road check to evaluate your vehicle's steering, suspension, clutch, transmission, driveline and other components. It will help determine whether the engine performs properly, and whether the brakes have enough stopping power. You can do a road check on the way to pick up the first passengers of the day.

Engine check

Be alert for any unusual engine noises, vibrations or lack of normal responses.

Test parking brake

To check this brake, try to move the vehicle forward slowly while the parking brake is on. If it moves easily, the parking brake is not holding properly and should be repaired. Note: Driving with the parking brake on is the most frequent cause of parking brake failure.

Check transmission operation

A manual transmission should allow for smooth, easy gear changes.

Standard transmission — check clutch

When starting an engine, the clutch pedal should be depressed to relieve the starter of the extra load of turning the transmission gears. The clutch should engage easily and smoothly without jerking, slipping excessively

or chattering. Never "ride" the clutch pedal. A properly adjusted clutch pedal should have some freeplay when the pedal is fully released.

While changing gears, carefully control the speed of the engine to shift without jerking or excessive clutch slippage. Erratic or careless gear shifting wears out the clutch.

Check the brakes

Test your brakes at low speeds, bringing the vehicle to a complete stop in a straight line. There should be no pulling to one side or excessive noise. Note any extra pedal pressure needed, or sponginess of the pedal. Do not drive the vehicle until problems have been repaired. If your vehicle is equipped with air brakes, please refer to The Air Brake Handbook.

Check the steering

Look for jerking or too much play in the system. Power steering should

15

be quiet, and the vehicle should steer easily in turns or when going over bumps. Look for unusual ride or handling.

Check the suspension

Broken springs, ruptured air bags and faulty shock absorbers may cause sag, bouncing, bottoming and excessive sway when driving.

Stay alert to the condition of your vehicle

Drivers should quickly sense the "thump-thumping" of a flat tire, or one that is under-inflated. Keep the right air pressure in the tires at all times to prevent premature tire wear, failure and breakdown. The air pressure in your spare tire should be the same as the pressure in the tire on the vehicle carrying the highest pressure. Again, recognize unusual noises or handling.

A vehicle should not be driven with any of these defects.

Chapter 1, section III — Summary

By the end of this section you should know:

- The qualifications and require-ments for a class C or F licence
- How to obtain a class C or F licence
- How to perform the daily trip inspection
- How to perform the daily road check

IV. School Bus Licence Classes B and E

A class B licence is needed to drive any school purposes bus having seats for more than twenty-four (24) passengers. It also allows you to operate vehicles included in classes C, D, E, F and G, but not motorcycles.

A class E licence is needed to drive any school purposes bus having seats for not more than twenty-four (24) passengers. It also allows you to operate vehicles included in classes F and G, but not motorcycles.

Definitions

Here are definitions of some words used in this section.

- **A bus:** a motor vehicle designed for carrying ten or more passengers and used for the transportation of persons.
- **A school purposes bus is:**
  - a bus while being operated by or under contract with a

school board or other authority in charge of a school for the transportation of adults with a developmental handicap or children; or

- a school bus, as defined in subsection 175 (1) of the Highway Traffic Act while being used for the transportation of adults with a developmental handicap or children.

- **A school bus:**
  - is painted chrome yellow, and
  - displays on the front and rear thereof the words "school bus" and on the rear thereof the words "do not pass when signals flashing".

- **A school purposes vehicle is:**
  - a station wagon, van or bus while being operated by or under contract with a school board or other authority in charge of a school for the transportation of adults with a developmental handicap or children; or

- a school bus as defined in subsection 175 (1) of the Highway Traffic Act.

- **Median strip:** a median is a physical barrier such as a raised, lowered, earth, or paved strip constructed to separate traffic travelling in different directions. Vehicles cannot cross over a median strip.

- **Highway:** a common and public highway, street, avenue, parkway, driveway, square, place, bridge, viaduct or trestle, any part of which is used by the public for the passage of vehicles, including the shoulders of the road and the land between property lines.

- **Roadway:** the part of the highway that is improved, designed or ordinarily used for traffic, not including the shoulder. Where a highway includes two or more separate roadways, the term roadway refers to any one roadway and not all of the roadways together.

Note: If you plan to operate a school bus or bus equipped with air brakes, you will need a Z endorsement on your licence. Please refer to the OFFICIAL AIR BRAKE HANDBOOK for more information.

Qualification requirements for classes B and E

An applicant for a class B or E driver's licence must:
- be at least 21 years of age;
- meet medical and vision standards;
- hold a valid Ontario class G or higher licence or equivalent issued in a province or territory of Canada;
- have successfully completed a school bus driver improvement course approved by the Minister and be able to show proof of successful completion with a valid course certificate (course certificates are valid for five years);
- have knowledge of bus equipment maintenance and passenger safety and control;

- pass an MTO driver examination or obtain a certificate of competence from a recognized authority by passing a vision screening, knowledge test and a driving test in a bus of appropriate size;
- not have accumulated more than six demerit points on his/her driving record;
- not have had a driver's licence under suspension at any time within the preceding 12 months as a result of having been convicted or found guilty of:
  - driving under suspension
  - speeding over 50 km above the limit
  - careless driving
  - racing on a highway
  - leaving the scene of an accident
  - a Criminal Code of Canada offence committed by means of a motor vehicle or while driving or having care and control of a motor vehicle

  - flight from police
- not have been convicted or found guilty within the preceding five years of two or more offences under the Criminal Code of Canada, committed on different dates by means of a motor vehicle, or while driving or having care and control of a motor vehicle
- not have been convicted or found guilty within the preceding five years under section 4 or 5 of The Narcotic Control Act of Canada
- not have been convicted or found guilty within the preceding five years of certain sexual or moral offences under the Criminal Code of Canada
- not have been convicted or found guilty of any offence for conduct that affords reasonable grounds for believing that he/she will not properly perform his/her duties, or is not a proper person to have custody of children

In addition, a holder of a class B or E driver's licence may not accumulate more than eight demerit points.

How to obtain a class B or E driver's licence

1. Pick up the necessary forms from any DriveTest Centre in Ontario, including the medical examination report form and study material.
2. Take the medical report to a physician of your choice. When the medical examination has been completed, return the report to the DriveTest Centre selected for your tests. Only applicants with satisfactory medical reports may take a knowledge test for a classified licence.
3. A criminal record search will be initiated when you pay your application fee.
4. You are required to pass the following:
   a) Vision screening
   b) Knowledge test including

a traffic signs recognition component and a test of operating knowledge of a school bus

c) Driving test in a vehicle of appropriate seating capacity

d) A satisfactory driver record search

5. Successfully complete a ministry approved school bus driver improvement course and obtain a certificate. School bus driver improvement course certificates are valid for five years.

Vision and knowledge test checklist, classes B and E

Before taking the class B or E knowledge test, make sure you have studied the Official Bus Handbook.

Bring the following items to the test:

- 2 pieces of identification or Ontario Driver's Licence
- Complete medical report form
- Money for test fees — cash, debit or credit card
- Glasses or contact lenses (if

you need to wear them to read or write)

Road test, classes B and E

On your class B or E road test —

- You will demonstrate a daily trip inspection, commonly known as a circle check. You will name the item of equipment checked and briefly describe its condition.
- You will drive in traffic and handle the vehicle safely according to the class of licence for which you are applying.
- You will demonstrate loading and unloading.
- You may be required to reverse the vehicle into a parking bay or marked area.
- You will demonstrate proper procedures at all railway crossings.

Road test checklist, classes B and E

Bring the following items to the road test:

- Appropriate vehicle in good working order
- Money for test fees (if applicable)
- Glasses (if you need to wear them to drive)
- Wheel chocks or blocks, if the vehicle is equipped with air brakes

Arrive at least 30 minutes before your road test appointment. All road tests have a set time frame. Before you begin your test, the examiner will inform you of the amount of time you have to complete it.

Daily trip inspection, classes B and E

Driver's circle check

A driver is not permitted to drive a bus, motor coach, school bus, or school purposes bus, van or station wagon unless the driver or another person has, within the previous 24 hours, conducted an inspection of the vehicle and completed an inspection report. The driver must continue to check all systems throughout the day because the condition of the vehicle can change. By staying alert, you can spot trouble before it causes a breakdown or collision.

The inspection is conducted in accordance with an inspection schedule. The schedule provides a list of vehicle systems and components that the driver is required to inspect and provides a list of defects to guide and assist the driver.

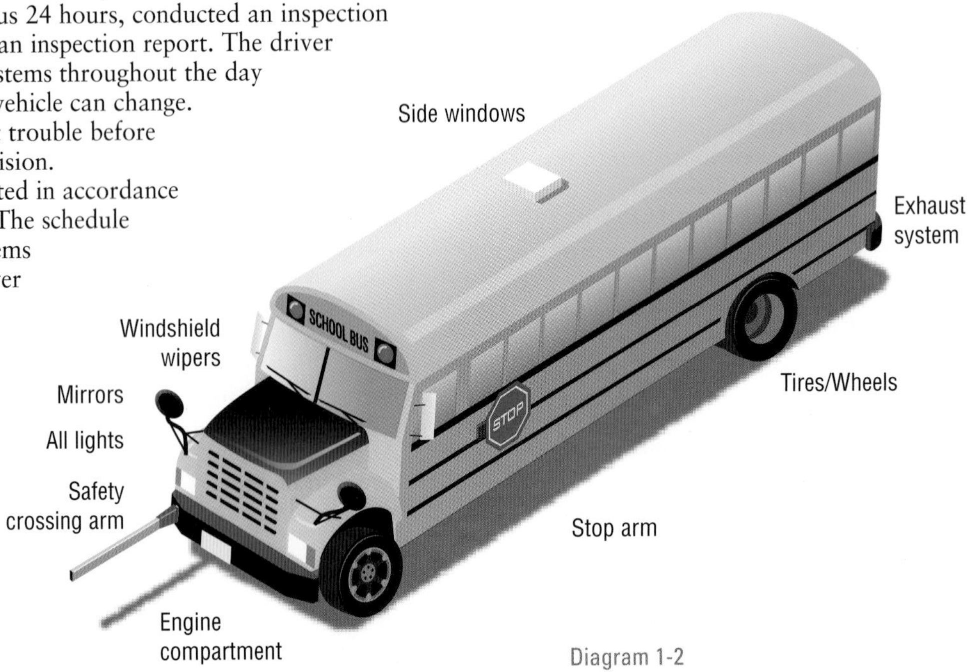

Side windows

Exhaust system

Windshield wipers

Mirrors

All lights

Safety crossing arm

Engine compartment

Tires/Wheels

Stop arm

SCHOOL BUS

STOP

Diagram 1-2

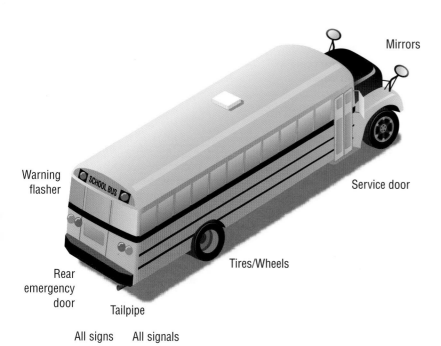

Mirrors

Warning
flasher

Service door

SCHOOL BUS

Tires/Wheels

Rear
emergency
door

Tailpipe

All signs   All signals

Diagram 1-3

The schedule used for the inspection depends upon the type of bus and its use as follows:

Schedule 2: buses, motor coaches, trailers towed by either vehicle

Schedule 5: yellow school buses, school-purposes buses

Schedule 6: school-purposes vans or station wagons when carrying six or more passengers

The inspection schedule divides defects into two categories, major and minor. When a minor defect is identified, the driver must record the defect on the inspection report and report the defect to the operator. Drivers are not permitted to drive a vehicle with a major defect.

Drivers must carry both the current inspection report and the applicable inspection schedule. Electronic reports and schedules are permitted.

The daily trip inspection or circle check in this book shows the absolute minimum inspection that must be performed as part of the driver testing procedure. For the full inspection schedules outlining all major and minor defects, which all commercial vehicle drivers are required to complete daily, refer to the Ontario Regulation 199/07 "Commercial Motor Vehicle Inspections" in the Highway Traffic Act at www.e-laws.gov.on.ca.

The law requires a vehicle transporting six or more children to and from school and operated by or under contract with a school board or other authority in charge of a school, to be equipped with a log book. (For more information, refer to section 4 of Regulation 612 on page 118.)

Outside inspection
- Alternating lights, front
- Headlights, directional signals, parking and clearance lights
- Windshield and wipers
- Engine compartment: fluid levels, wiring, belts, hoses and hydraulic brake fluid leaks (if so equipped)
- Tires (retreads on rear wheels only)
- Exposed wheel nuts, lugs and studs
- Exhaust system for leaks
- Directional, stop tail and clearance lights
- Emergency exit
- Alternating lights, rear
- Rear windows (for cleanliness) if applicable
- Entrance door
- Body condition (for sharp edges)
- Fuel system (tank, cap, and for leaks)
- Signs (for cleanliness and legibility)
- Stop Arm

Inside inspection
- Steering wheel (for excessive freeplay)
- Brake pedal reserve and fade
- Brake booster operation
- Brake failure warning light
- Parking brake operation
- Brake air pressure or vacuum gauge
- Warning signal, low air pressure/vacuum
- Interior (for exhaust fumes)
- Signal and hazard lights, switch and pilot
- Alternating lights, switch and signal device
- Interior lights
- Windshield washer and wipers
- Windshield and windows
- Mirrors, adjustment and condition
- Defroster and heaters
- Horn
- Stop arm mechanism
- Driver's seat belt and seat security
- Service door and controls
- Passengers' seat security

- Emergency exit and warning signal
- Floor covering (tripping hazards)
- Fire extinguisher
- Axe or claw bar
- First aid kit
- Flares or reflectors
- Interior (for cleanliness)
- Passenger seat belts (if so equipped)

Final check before driving onto the highway:

- Driver's seat belt fastened
- Drive forward and brake to a stop to test the service brake
- Additional check of all gauges — heat, oil and vacuum, etc.
- Complete log book entry

NOTE: If this type of vehicle is being used for other than a school purposes vehicle, the daily trip inspection used will be the one on pages 13 to 15 for coaches.

The daily road check (while driving the vehicle)

Drivers are required to examine and observe the condition of the vehicle

during the day or trip. Plan a road check to evaluate your vehicle's steering, suspension, clutch, transmission, driveline and other components to determine whether the engine performs properly, and whether the brakes have enough stopping power.

You can do a road check on the way to pick up the first passengers of the day.

Check the suspension

Broken springs, ruptured air bags and faulty shock absorbers may cause sag, bouncing, bottoming and excessive sway when under way.

Engine check

Be alert for any unusual engine noises, vibrations or lack of normal responses.

Check the steering

Look for jerking or excessive play in the system. Power steering should be quiet, and the vehicle should steer easily in turns or when going

over bumps. Look for unusual ride or handling.

Check transmission and clutch

A manual transmission should allow for smooth, easy gear changes.

The clutch should engage easily and smoothly without jerking, slipping excessively or chattering. Never "ride" the clutch pedal. A properly adjusted clutch pedal should have some "freeplay" when the pedal is fully released.

While changing gears, carefully control the speed of the engine to shift without jerking or excessive clutch slippage. Erratic or careless gear shifting wears out the clutch.

Test parking brake

To check this brake, try to move the vehicle forward slowly while the parking brake is on. If it moves easily, the parking brake is not holding properly and should be repaired.

Check the brakes

Test at low speeds, bringing the vehicle to a complete stop. The vehicle should stop in a straight line. There should be no pulling to one side or excessive noise. Note any extra pedal pressure or sponginess. Do not operate the vehicle until such conditions have been repaired.

Note: Driving with the parking brake on is the most frequent cause of parking brake failure.

Stay alert to the condition of your vehicle

Drivers should quickly sense the "thump-thumping" of a flat tire, or one that is underinflated. Keep the right air pressure in the tires to prevent premature tire wear, failure and breakdown. The air pressure in your spare tire should be the same as the pressure in the tire on the vehicle carrying the highest pressure. Again, recognize unusual noises or handling. A vehicle should not be driven with any of these defects.

Chapter 1, section IV — Summary

By the end of this section you should know:

- The qualifications and requirements for a class B or E licence
- How to obtain a class B or E licence
- How to perform the daily trip inspection
- How to perform the daily road check

Chapter 2

Defensive driving

The most important concern to a bus driver is the safety of the passengers. Professional drivers who carry passengers must observe the rules of the road, understand and practice defensive driving, and take special precautions in loading and unloading.

The professional looks ahead, thinks ahead, acts early and drives defensively. A person who drives defensively:

- Keeps space around the vehicle
- Keeps his or her eyes moving and sees what is happening far ahead and to the sides
- Checks the mirrors frequently
- Recognizes possible danger far enough in advance to take preventive action
- Makes allowances for the errors of other drivers and pedestrians
- Gives up the right-of-way if it will avoid possible danger to the driver or passengers
- Makes allowances for the rapidly changing conditions of the road, weather and traffic
- Shows courtesy to other road users
- Wears a seat belt
- Uses headlights at all times to make sure the bus is easily seen
- Drives at a safe speed, slowing when road conditions call for longer stopping distance and greater control

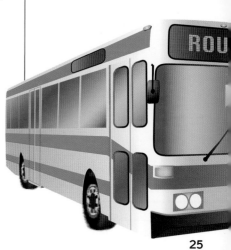

10 ways you can help make Ontario's roads the safest in North America

1. Don't drink and drive. Don't drive when you're taking medication that will affect your driving.

2. Wear your seat belt. (Unless you are a passenger on a bus without seat belts).

3. Obey the speed limits. Slow down when road and weather conditions are poor.

4. Don't take risks: don't cut people off in traffic, make sudden lane changes or run yellow lights.

5. Don't drive when you're tired, upset or sick.

6. If you're in doubt, let the other driver go first — yield the right-of-way.

7. Keep a safe distance between your vehicle and the one ahead.

8. Avoid distractions such as loud music and CB radios.

9. Check your mirrors frequently; always check your blind spot before you change lanes.

10. Check traffic in all directions before going into an intersection.

I. Driving techniques

Diagram 2-1

Steering (forward) and off track

The rear wheels of the vehicle do not pivot and so will not follow the same path as the front wheels. In a curve, the greater the distance (wheel base) between the front wheels and the rear wheels of the vehicle, the greater the amount of "off-track". The off track path of the rear wheels is closer to the curb than the path of the front wheels.

On the highway, you must lead your turning arc of the front wheels according to the sharpness of the curve and your vehicle's off track. On a curve to the right keep the front wheels close to the centre line to prevent dropping the rear wheels off the pavement.

On a curve to the left, keep the front wheels closer to the right edge of the pavement to prevent the rear wheels from crossing into the other traffic lane.

Whenever possible, make turns from the proper lanes. When you must use portions of another lane to make sharp turns, it is your responsibility to be sure that such a move can be made safely, without interfering with other road users (Diagram 2-1).

Steering while reversing

When backing, use all rear view mirrors. Back slowly even with two or three mirrors, because your vision to the rear is limited. There is always a blind spot to the rear that a mirror cannot reflect.

When you have no observer, you should leave the vehicle and check the path that it will take before attempting to back up.

Right turns

Right turns with vehicles that have a lot of off track require the driver to lead the turning arc according to the amount of off track. Running the rear wheels of the vehicle over curbs and sidewalks is dangerous and may cause damage to the

27

Diagram 2-2

suspension, wheels and tires. You must be careful not to hit objects such as power poles, sign posts or lamp standards mounted close to the curb. Generally, it is better to use

more space from the road you are entering than from the road you are leaving.

In narrow streets, proceed well into the intersection before turning the steering wheel. You may need to travel partially over the centre line of the street entered or into the second traffic lane. If so, you must use extreme caution and make sure you can move safely. When you have to partially block off another lane in this manner, make sure that smaller vehicles such as motorcycles and bicycles are not moving up on your right side. Remember, your ability to see is restricted when you are in the middle of a turn (Diagram 2-2).

Left turns

Be aware of any off tracking when making a left turn. Unless you use your left outside mirror to monitor the path of the rear wheels, those wheels may hit a vehicle or a sign post on an island. You must turn the

vehicle in a wide arc before bringing it back to its proper position after a left turn, just right of the centre line. Then as you speed up, you can move, when it is safe, to the right lane (Diagram 2-3).

Brake inspection

While you are not expected to be able to repair your brakes, you should be able to tell when there is a problem. Use the following inspection routine as part of your daily trip inspection.

1. Hydraulic brakes (without power assist):
   a) Apply brakes moderately and hold.
   b) If the pedal shows a steady drop, the vehicle should be taken out of service and the system inspected professionally.
2. Hydraulic brakes (with power assist):
   a) With the engine stopped, pump the brake pedal several times to eliminate power assist.

Diagram 2-3

b) Apply brakes moderately and hold.

c) Start the engine (the pedal should drop slightly) and stop.

d) If the pedal continues to drop or does not drop (no power assist) stop the engine. The vehicle should be taken out of service and the system inspected professionally.

Use of brakes

Apply brakes with steady pressure at the beginning of a stop, then ease off as the vehicle slows. Just before the vehicle comes to a complete stop, release brakes to avoid jerk and rebound, then brake again to hold the vehicle while stopped.

Hydraulic brakes or air brakes should not be fanned (alternately applied and released) except on slippery pavement where this type of braking (called threshold braking) may give better control, reduce the danger of skidding and give a shorer stop. However, fanning air brakes may sharply reduce air pressure. Fanning serves no useful purpose on dry pavement and, on a long downhill grade, may reduce air pressure below the minimum pressure needed for stopping the vehicle.

Avoid excessive use of brakes on long downgrades as overheated brakes are dangerously inefficient. Gear down to use engine compression as the principal means of controlling speed on long grades. You should use the same gear going down a long grade as you would to climb it. Choose the lower gear before you begin going downhill.

If the low air pressure warning device operates at any time, stop immediately in the safest available place and have the problem corrected before you proceed.

If your brakes fail on a level road, down-shift (manual or automatic) and use engine compression to slow the vehicle. In an emergency, it may be necessary to use the emergency brake. Do not drive the vehicle again until repairs have been made.

Take care when braking on a wet or slippery surface or on a curve. Late or over-braking in these circumstances could cause skidding. To stop a skid, release the brakes, look and steer in the direction you want to go.

Retarders have become a popular option on motor coaches. They augment braking and help reduce service brake wear and brake fade, and are useful on long downhill grades.

There are three types of brake retarders: exhaust brakes, engine brakes, and driveline (transmission) retarders. Activation of the retarder is usually controlled by the driver by means of an "on-off" or variable set-ting switch. In some buses, the retarder activates automatically when the service brakes are applied. Exhaust and engine brake retarders typically increase engine noise and many communities prohibit their use.

Always respect signs advising against the use of engine or exhaust brakes. Driveline retarders don't increase engine noise. However, prolonged use increases transmission heat to the point that it could shut down the coach to protect the transmission from damage.

Warning: Because the retarder applies brake force only to the drive axle, activating the retarder while driving on a slippery surface can cause a loss of control and a collision. Do not use the retarder on wet, slippery or icy roads. During inclement weather, turn off the retarder using the maters (on-off) switch. Drivers who ignore this warning and experience a retarder-induced wheel lock-up or spin should immediately turn off the retarder to allow the drive wheels to roll freely and regain steering control.

Note: If you plan to operate a vehicle equipped with air brakes, refer to the OFFICIAL AIR BRAKE HANDBOOK for more information.

Following distance

Commercial motor vehicles must keep a minimum distance of at least 60 m (200 ft) between themselves and other vehicles when on a highway at a speed over 60 km/h (40 mph) except when overtaking and passing another vehicle.

Stopping at Railway Crossings

All railway crossings on public roads in Ontario are marked with red and white "X" signs. Watch for these signs and be prepared to stop. You may also see yellow advance warning signs and pavement markings of a large X at approaches to railway crossings. Some railway crossings have flashing signal lights while some use gates or barriers to keep motorists from crossing the tracks when a train is coming.

All buses and other public vehicles are required to stop at railway crossings that do not have automatic warning devices such as barriers and signal lights. School buses must stop at all railway crossings whether or not they have automatic warning devices. Motorists must be prepared to stop behind these vehicles. Obey all signs and signals. Remember — it can take up to two kilometres for a train to stop under full emergency braking.

When you come to a railway crossing, remember:

- Slow down, listen and look both ways to make sure the way is clear before crossing the tracks.
- If a train is coming, stop at least five metres from the nearest rail or gate. Do not cross the track until you are sure the train or trains have passed.
- Never race a train to a crossing.
- If there are signal lights, wait until they stop flashing and, if the crossing has a gate or barrier, wait until it rises, before you cross the tracks.
- Never drive around, under, or through a railway gate or barrier while it is down, being lowered, or being raised. It is illegal and dangerous.
- Never stop in the middle of railway tracks. For example, in heavy traffic, make sure you have enough room to cross the tracks completely before you begin to cross.
- Don't shift gears while crossing tracks.
- If you get trapped on a crossing, immediately get everyone out and away from the vehicle. Move to a safe place and then contact authorities.

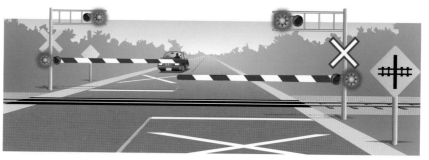

Diagram 2-4

- Buses and other public vehicles are required to stop at railway crossings that are not protected by gates, signal lights, or a stop sign. School buses must stop at railway crossings whether or not they are protected by gates or signal lights. Watch for these buses and be prepared to stop behind them.
- If you are approaching a railway crossing with a stop sign, you must stop unless otherwise directed by a flagman.

For laws relating to school buses stopping at railway crossings, see pages 113 to 114.

II. Sharing the road

Sharing the road with smaller vehicles

Be aware that most drivers of smaller vehicles do not understand what it is like to drive a vehicle such as a tractor trailer or bus. Many do not realize that some large vehicles need twice as much stopping distance as the average car, and takes much longer to get up to normal driving speed. Many drivers also feel nervous when a large vehicle comes up behind or beside them, and this may cause them to make sudden or unexpected moves.

Here are some tips for sharing the road with smaller vehicles:

1. **Following** — It is very dangerous to follow to closely behind another vehicle. If something unexpected occurs, you will not have enough room to stop safely. Also, be aware that a large vehicle looming up closely behind may intimidate drivers of small vehicles.
2. **Being Passed** — Be courteous when smaller, faster vehicles

are trying to pass you. Slow down enough to allow the vehicle to fit in quickly and safely in front of you.
3. **Signalling** — Signal your intentions clearly before turning, slowing or stopping so that other drivers will have adequate time to react appropriately.
4. **Turning** — Many drivers of smaller vehicles do not understand how much room large vehicles need in order to make a turn. Drivers of smaller vehicles will often drive up into the large vehicle's turning space, not realizing until too late that the large vehicle needs that space to complete the turn. Always check to make sure a vehicle has not moved up into your turning space before completing your turn.

Sharing the road with motorcycles, limited-speed motorcycles or mopeds

Motorcycles, limited-speed motorcycles and mopeds are harder to see because of their size. Drivers of these vehicles may make sudden moves because of uneven road surfaces or poor weather conditions. Because they are less protected, they are more likely to be injured in a collision.

Motorcycles and mopeds that cannot keep up with traffic should drive as close as possible to the right edge of the road; however, remember that these vehicles have the right to use the whole lane.

Since many motorcycle turn signals do not automatically shut off, be careful when turning left in front of an oncoming motorcycle with its turn signal on. Make sure the motorcyclist is actually turning; he or she may have just forgotten to switch off the turn signal.

Sharing the road with cyclists

Bicycles and mopeds that cannot keep up with traffic are expected to keep to the right of the lane; how-ever, they can use any part of the lane if necessary for safety, such as to avoid potholes and sewer grates. Cyclists need a metre on either side of themselves as a safety zone. When passing a cyclist, allow at least one metre between your vehicle and the cyclist. If the lane is too narrow to share, change lanes to pass the cyclist. When turning right, signal and check your mirrors and the blind spot to your right to make sure you do not cut off a cyclist. When parked on the side of the street, look behind you and check your mirrors and blinds spots for a passing cyclist before opening a door.

Sharing the road with farm machinery

Farm machinery moves quite slowly compared to other road users. Most tractors and combines have a maximum speed of 40 km/h, but travel at less than 40 km/h when towing implements or wagons. Farm machinery is often oversized,

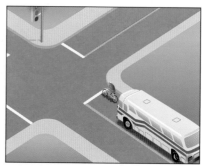
Diagram 2-5

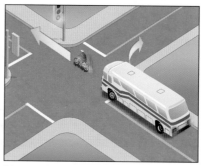
Diagram 2-6

wide or long or both, making it difficult for the driver to see vehicles coming up from behind. Farmers often turn directly into fields rather than roads or lanes, or move from lane to lane. Remember that it is common for farmers to be on the roads after dark during peak planting and harvesting seasons.

Farm machinery on the road must display an orange and red slow-moving vehicle sign on the rear of the vehicle. The sign warns other drivers that the vehicle is travelling at 40 km/h or less. If you see one of these signs, slow down and be cautious. Stay well back and do not pass until it is safe to do so. (See the slow-moving vehicle sign on page 73.)

Sharing the road with pedestrians

Pay special attention to pedestrians, whether they are crossing roads in traffic, walking or jogging alongside roads, or using crosswalks or crossovers (generally known as crossings). Watch for children. Drive slowly and cautiously through school zones, residential areas and any other area where children may be walking or playing. You never know when a child might dart out from between parked cars or try to cross a street without checking for oncoming traffic. Be very cautious at twilight when children may still be playing outside, but are very difficult to see. Watch out for Community Safety Zone signs as they indicate areas where the community has identified that there is a special risk to pedestrians.

Elderly pedestrians, or those with disabilities, need extra caution and courtesy from drivers, as they may be slow in crossing the road. Be alert for pedestrians who are blind, visually impaired, hearing impaired, people in wheelchairs or people walking slowly due to some other physical impairment and give them appropriate consideration. Pedestrians who are blind or visually impaired may use a white cane or guide dog to help them travel safely along sidewalks and across intersections. Caution signs are posted in some areas where there is a special need for drivers to be alert.

Persons operating mobility devices (motorized wheelchair and medical scooters) are treated the same way as pedestrians. Usually these operators will travel along a sidewalk but if there is no sidewalk available, persons using a mobility device should travel, like pedestrians, along the left shoulder of the roadway facing oncoming traffic.

Some streetcar stops have a special safety island or zone for passengers getting on and off. Pass these safety islands and zones at a reasonable speed. Always be ready in case pedestrians make sudden or unexpected moves.

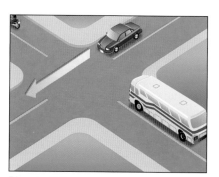

Diagram 2-7
Yielding the right-of-way
There are times when you must yield the right-of-way. This means you must let another person go first. Here are some rules about when you must yield the right-of-way:

At an intersection without signs or lights, you must yield the right-of-way to any vehicle approaching from the right (Diagram 2-7).

At an intersection with stop signs at all corners, you must yield the right-of-way to the first vehicle to come to a complete stop. If two

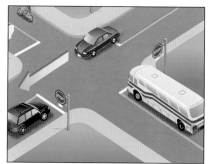

Diagram 2-8
vehicles stop at the same time, the vehicle on the left must yield to the vehicle on the right (Diagram 2-8).

At any intersection where you want to turn left or right, you must yield the right-of-way. If you are turning left, you must wait for approaching traffic to pass or turn and for pedestrians in your path to cross. If you are turning right, you must wait for pedestrians to cross (Diagram 2-9).

A yield sign means you must slow down or stop if necessary and yield the right-of-way to traffic

Diagram 2-9
in the intersection or on the intersecting road.

When entering a road from a private road or driveway, you must yield to vehicles on the road and pedestrians on the sidewalk (Diagram 2-10).

You must yield the right-of-way to pedestrians crossing at specially marked pedestrian crossings or crossovers (Diagram 2-11).

Remember, signalling does not give you the right-of-way. You must make sure the way is clear.

Diagram 2-10

Diagram 2-11

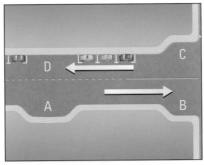

Diagram 2-12

A Mid-block indented bays
B An indentation before an intersection
C An indentation after an intersection
D Bus stops between legally parked cars

Municipal bus bays

Many municipal roadways have special indented stopping areas for municipal buses, called bus bays, where passengers can get on and off. There are three types of bus bays:

- Mid-block indented bays
- Indentations immediately before and after intersections
- Bus stop areas between two designated parking areas (Diagram 2-12)

When a bus in a bus bay begins flashing its left turn signals, indicating that it is ready to leave the bus bay, and you are approaching in the lane adjacent to the bus bay, you must allow the bus to re-enter traffic.

If you are a bus driver re-entering traffic from a bus bay, flash your left turn signals to indicate that you are ready to leave the bus bay. This tells other drivers who are approaching in the lane adjacent to the bus bay that you are going to re-enter traffic. Proceed with caution.

III. Hours of Service

As of January 1, 2007, new hours of service came into effect for all drivers of commercial motor vehicles. This section provides an overview of the basic rules. All the details of the hours of service requirements are contained in the Highway Traffic Act in Ontario Regulation 555/06.

The Hours of Service regulations apply to drivers of the following types of vehicles:

- Commercial motor vehicles having gross weight or registered gross weight over 4,500 kilograms
- Buses, school buses and school-purposes buses

Exemptions to Hours of Service regulations

Drivers of the following types of vehicles are not required to comply with the Hours of Service regulations:

- Commercial motor vehicles, other than buses, having gross weight or registered gross weight of not more than 4,500 kilograms

- Commercial motor vehicles leased for no longer than thirty days by an individual
- Commercial motor vehicles, operated under dealer or service permits, that are not transporting passengers or goods
- Commercial motor vehicles operated under the authority of In-Transit permits
- Two or three axle commercial motor vehicles transporting primary farm, forest, sea or lake products
- Mobile cranes
- Pick-up trucks, being used for personal purposes, which have a manufacturer's gross vehicle weight rating of 6,000 kilograms or less
- Tow trucks
- Motor homes
- Municipal buses operated as part of a public transit service
- Buses used for personal purposes without compensation
- Vehicles being used by a police officers

- Cardiac arrest vehicles
- Vehicles engaged in providing relief in emergencies
- Ambulances, fire apparatus, hearses or casket wagons

Duty Status

The new rules define four categories of duty time for commercial vehicle drivers:

- Off-duty time, other than time spent in a sleeper berth
- Off-duty time spent in a sleeper berth
- On-duty time spent driving
- On-duty time, other than time spent driving

On duty activities include driving, as well as performing any other activities for the operator, such as inspecting, cleaning or repairing your vehicle; travelling as a co-driver (not including when in sleeper berth); loading and unloading the vehicle; waiting at inspections, for unloading or loading to be completed, or because of an unforeseen occurrence such as an accident.

These four categories are used to determine the minimum off-duty hours required and the maximum on-duty hours allowed for commercial vehicle drivers.

Hours of service requirements

1. Daily requirement*

- A driver must have 10 hours off-duty in a day.
- A driver cannot drive more than 13 hours in a day.
- A driver cannot drive after 14 hours on-duty in a day.

* Some exceptions apply, refer to Ontario Regulation 555/06.

2. Mandatory off-duty time

- After a period of at least 8 hours off-duty, a driver cannot drive more than 13 hours.
- After a period of at least 8 hours off-duty, a driver cannot drive after having been on-duty for 14 hours.

- After a period of at least 8 hours off-duty, a driver cannot drive after 16 hours has elapsed.

3. Cycle requirement

- An operator shall designate a cycle for the driver to follow.
- There are two cycles available, a 7-day cycle or a 14-day cycle.
- In a period of 7 consecutive days, a driver cannot drive after having been on-duty for 70 hours.
- In a period of 14 consecutive days, a driver cannot drive after having been on-duty for 120 hours. Drivers following this cycle shall not drive after accumulating 70 hours on-duty without having taken 24 consecutive hours of off-duty time.
- On any day, all drivers must have a period of at least 24 consecutive hours off-duty in the preceding 14 days.

4. Cycle reset/switching

- A driver may only switch the cycle they are on if they start a new cycle.

- To start a new cycle, a driver on the 7-day cycle must take 36 consecutive hours off-duty.
- To start a new cycle, a driver on the 14-day cycle must take 72 consecutive hours off-duty.

5. Daily log requirement

A daily log may be handwritten, computer generated or made by means of a recording device. The daily log must contain the following information:

- The driver's name
- The date
- The name of the driver's co-drivers, if any
- The start time of the day being recorded, if the day does not start at midnight
- The cycle that the driver is following
- The odometer reading, at the start of the day
- The number plate of each commercial motor vehicle to be driven and each trailer

- The name of the operator
- The address of the driver's home terminal and of the principal place of business of the operator
- Graph grid as illustrated in Form 1 of the regulation (not required for Recording Device)
- The start and end times for each duty status during the day
- The location where the driver's duty status changes
- The total time spent in each duty status during the day
- The odometer reading at the end of the day
- The total distance driven by the driver
- The driver's signature

Daily log exemption

A driver is not required to keep a daily log if the driver:

1. Drives the commercial motor vehicle solely within a radius of 160 kilometres of the location at which the driver starts the day
2. Returns at the end of the day to the same location from which he or she started
3. Only works for one operator that day

If a driver is not required to keep a daily log the operator shall keep a record for the day showing:

- The date, driver's name and the location where the driver starts and ends the day
- The cycle that the driver is following
- The hour at which each duty status starts and ends
- The total number of hours spent in each duty status

These rules will help keep Ontario's roads safe by allowing commercial drivers to get the rest they need in order to safely operate their vehicles. For more details about the hours of service requirements, visit the MTO website at www.mto.gov.on.ca, or refer to the Highway Traffic Act at www.e-laws.gov.on.ca.

Chapter 2 — Summary

By the end of this chapter you should know:

- The concept of defensive driving
- How to steer in forward, reverse and while turning
- The meaning of "off track" and where to position your vehicle on the road
- The importance of sharing the road with other road users especially small vehicles, farm machinery, cyclists and pedestrians
- The concept of right of way and common situations where you must yield to other road users
- The rules for hours of service

Chapter 3

Driving a bus is a specialized skill that requires you to be alert to what is happening on the inside and outside of the vehicle. Here are some items to keep in mind before you start out:

Special precautions

- Starting and stopping a vehicle should be a smooth, gradual operation. With a manual transmission, use the hand brake to hold the vehicle while co-ordinating the clutch and accelerator. This helps prevent rolling back on an upgrade. Thinking ahead can eliminate the need for sudden stops.
- Bad weather requires all drivers to adjust their driving habits and take extra care. Noise, worries and other distractions slow down a driver's ability to react. Slow down and keep more clear space around the vehicle. A vehicle with manual (standard) transmission and conventional tires may start a great deal easier on icy roads if you place the gear selector lever in second gear.
- Think ahead and prepare for hazards such as narrow or rough roads, sharp turns, narrow bridges and severe dust — slow down.
- Ventilate and heat the vehicle when necessary.
- Close and secure all doors when the vehicle is moving.
- Never permit an unauthorized person to sit in the driver's seat, operate the vehicle, or any of its controls.
- Do not allow passengers to obstruct the vision of the driver to the front, sides or rear.
- Never load the vehicle beyond its licensed capacity. (This does not apply to city buses which are allowed to operate over seated capacity with no limit on standees.)

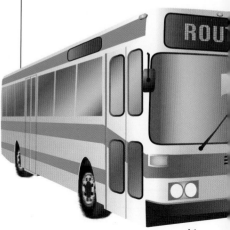

- Except when passing, keep 60 metres (200 ft) between buses travelling in the same direction on a highway outside a city, town or village.

I. Driving at night and in bad weather

At night and in weather conditions such as rain, snow or fog, you cannot see as far ahead, even with headlights. Slow down when driving at night, especially on unlit roads, and whenever weather conditions reduce your visibility.

Overdriving your headlights

You are overdriving your headlights when your stopping distance is farther than you can see with your headlights. This is a dangerous thing to do because you may not give yourself enough room to make a safe stop. Reflective road signs can mislead you as well, making you believe you can see farther than you really can. This may cause you to overdrive your headlights if you are not careful.

Glare

Glare is dazzling light that makes it hard for you to see and be aware of what others around you are doing.

It can be a problem on both sunny and overcast days, depending on the angle of the sun's rays and your surroundings. Glare can also be a problem at night when you face bright headlights or see them reflected in your mirrors.

When meeting oncoming vehicles with bright headlights at night, look up and beyond and slightly to the right of the oncoming lights. In daytime glare, use your sun visor or use a pair of good quality sunglasses. When you enter a tunnel on a bright day, slow down to let your eyes adjust to the reduced light. Remove sunglasses when you are driving through a tunnel.

Cut down glare at night by following the rules of the road for vehicle lights. Use your lowbeam headlights within 150 metres (500 ft) of an oncoming vehicle or when following a vehicle within 60 metres (200 ft). On country roads, switch to lowbeams when you come to a curve or hilltop so you can see oncoming headlights and won't blind oncoming drivers.

Fog

Fog is a thin layer of cloud resting on the ground. Fog reduces visibility for drivers, resulting in difficult driving conditions. The best thing to do is to avoid driving in fog. Check weather forecasts and if there is a fog warning, delay your trip until it clears. If that is not possible or if you get caught driving in fog, there are a number of safe driving tips you should follow. If visibility is decreasing rapidly, move off the road and into a safe parking area to wait for the fog to lift.

Tips for driving safely in fog

Before you drive — and during your trip — check weather forecasts. If there is a fog warning, delay your trip until it clears, if possible. If you are caught driving in fog, follow these safe driving tips:

DO:

- Slow down gradually and drive at a speed that suits the conditions.
- Make sure the full lighting system of your vehicle is turned on.
- Use your lowbeam headlights Highbeams reflect off the moisture droplets in the fog, making it harder to see.
- If you have fog lights on your vehicle, use them, in addition to your lowbeams. They could save your life.
- Be patient. Avoid passing, changing lanes and crossing traffic.
- Use pavement markings to help guide you. Use the right edge of the road as a guide, rather than the centre line.

- Increase your following distance. You will need extra distance to brake safely.
- Look and listen for any hazards that may be ahead.
- Reduce the distractions in your vehicle. For example, turn off the cell phone. Your full attention is required.
- Watch for any electronically-operated warning signs.
- Keep looking as far ahead as possible.
- Keep your windows and mirrors clean. Use your defroster and wipers to maximize your vision.
- If the fog is too dense to continue, pull completely off the road and try to position your vehicle in a safe parking area. Turn on your emergency flashers.

DON'T:

- Don't stop on the travelled portion of the road. You could become

the first link in a chain-reaction collision.
- Don't speed up suddenly, even if the fog seems to be clearing. You could find yourself suddenly back in fog.
- Don't speed up to pass a vehicle moving slowly or to get away from a vehicle that is following too closely.

REMEMBER:

- Watch your speed. You may be going faster than you think. If so, reduce speed gradually.
- Leave a safe braking distance between you and the vehicle ahead.
- Remain calm and patient. Don't pass other vehicles or speed up suddenly.
- Don't stop on the road. If visibility is decreasing rapidly, pull off the road into a safe parking area and wait for the fog to lift.
- When visibility is reduced, use your lowbeam lights.

Rain

Rain makes road surfaces slippery, especially as the first drops fall. With more rain, tires make less contact with the road. If there is too much water or if you are going too fast, your tires may ride on top of the water, like water skis. This is called hydroplaning. When this happens, control becomes very difficult. Make sure you have good tires with deep tread, and slow down when the road is wet.

Rain also reduces visibility. Drive slow enough to be able to stop within the distance you can see. Make sure your windshield wipers are in good condition. If your wiper blades do not clean the windshield without streaking, replace them.

In rain, try to drive on clear sections of road. Look ahead and plan your movements. Smooth steering, braking and accelerating will reduce the chance of skids. Leave more space between you and the vehicle ahead in case you have to stop. This will also help you to avoid spray from the vehicle ahead that can make it even harder to see.

Avoid driving in puddles. A puddle can hide a large pothole that could damage your vehicle or its suspension, or flatten a tire. The spray of water could splash nearby pedestrians or drown your engine, causing it to stall. Water can also make your brakes less effective.

Flooded roads

Avoid driving on flooded roads — water may prevent your brakes from working. If you must drive through a flooded stretch of road, test your brakes afterwards to dry them out.

Test your brakes when it is safe to do so by stopping quickly and firmly. Make sure the vehicle stops in a straight line, without pulling to one side. The brake pedal should feel firm and secure, not spongy — that's a sign of trouble. If you still feel a pulling to one side or a spongy brake pedal even after the brakes are dry, you should take the vehicle in for repair immediately.

Skids

Once in a skid, look where you want your vehicle to go and steer in that direction. Most skids result from driving too fast for road or traffic conditions. Sudden, hard braking, going too fast around a corner or accelerating too quickly can cause your vehicle to skid or roll over.

Once in a skid, look where you want the vehicle to go and steer in that direction. Be careful not to oversteer. If you are on ice, skidding in a straight line, step on the clutch or shift to neutral.

- **Threshold Braking** — Threshold braking should bring you to a reasonably quick controlled stop in your own lane, even in slippery conditions. Brake as hard as you can without locking up or skidding the wheels. Press down on the brake pedal, trying to get as much braking power as possible. Then, if you feel any of the wheels locking up, release the brake pressure slightly and re-apply. Don't pump the brakes. Continue braking this way until you have brought the vehicle to a complete stop. Some vehicles have anti-lock brake systems that give you a maximum threshold stop automatically.

- **Anti-lock brakes** — Anti-lock braking systems (ABS) are designed to sense the speed of the wheels on a vehicle. An abnormal drop in wheel speed, which indicates potential wheel lock, causes the brake force to be reduced to that wheel. This is how the anti-lock braking system prevents tire skid and the accompanying loss of steering control. This improves vehicle safety during heavy brake use or when braking with poor traction.

If your vehicle has an anti-lock braking system, practice emergency braking to understand how your vehicle will react. Drivers unfamiliar with anti-lock braking are usually surprised by the vibration that happens the first time they must brake hard in an emergency. Make sure you know what to expect so you can react quickly and effectively in an emergency. It is a good idea to practice doing this under controlled conditions with a qualified driving instructor.

Although anti-lock braking systems help to prevent wheel lock, you should not expect the stopping distance for your vehicle to be shortened. Under normal driving conditions, on clean dry roads, you will notice no difference between vehicles with anti-lock braking and vehicles without anti-lock braking.

Snow

Snow may be hard-packed and slippery as ice; rutted and full of tracks and gullies; or, it can be smooth and soft. Look ahead and anticipate what you must do based on the conditions. Slow down on rutted snowy roads. Avoid sudden steering, braking or accelerating that could cause a skid.

Whiteouts

Blowing snow may create whiteouts, which is when snow completely blocks your view of the road. When blowing snow is forecast, drive only if necessary and with extreme caution.

Tips for driving in blowing snow and whiteout conditions

Before you drive — and during your trip — check weather forecasts and road reports. If there is a weather warning, or reports of poor visibility and driving conditions, delay your trip until conditions improve, if possible. If you get caught driving in blowing snow or a whiteout, follow these safe driving tips:

DO:
- Slow down gradually and drive at a speed that suits the conditions.
- Make sure the full lighting system of your vehicle is turned on.
- Be patient. Avoid passing, changing lanes and crossing traffic.
- Increase your following distance. You will need extra space to brake safely.
- Stay alert. Keep looking as far ahead as possible.
- Reduce the distractions in your vehicle. Your full attention is required.

- Keep your windows and mirrors clean. Use defroster and wipers to maximize your vision.
- Try to get off the road when visibility is near zero. Pull into a safe parking area if possible.

DON'T:
- Don't stop on the travelled portion of the road. You could become the first link in a chain-reaction collision.
- Don't attempt to pass a vehicle moving slowly or speed up to get away from a vehicle that is following too closely.

REMEMBER:
- Watch your speed. You may be going faster than you think. If so, reduce speed gradually.
- Leave a safe braking distance between you and the vehicle ahead.

- Stay alert, remain calm and be patient.
- If visibility is decreasing rapidly, do not stop on the road. Look for an opportunity to pull off the road into a safe parking area and wait for conditions to improve.
- If you become stuck or stranded in severe weather, stay with your vehicle for warmth and safety until help arrives. Open a window slightly for ventilation. Run your motor sparingly. Use your emergency flashers.
- Be prepared and carry a winter driving survival kit that includes items such as warm clothing, non-perishable energy foods, flashlight, shovel and blanket.
- It is important to look ahead and watch for clues that indicate you need to slow down and anticipate slippery road conditions.

Ice

As temperatures drop below freezing, wet roads become icy. Sections of road in shaded areas or on bridges and overpasses freeze first. It is important to look ahead, slow down and anticipate ice.

If the road ahead looks like black and shiny asphalt, be suspicious. It may be covered by a thin layer of ice known as black ice. Generally, asphalt in the winter should look gray-white in colour. If you think there may be black ice ahead, slow down and be careful.

Snow plows

Snow removal vehicles are equipped with flashing blue lights that can be seen from 150 metres (500 ft).

Flashing blue lights warn you of wide and slow-moving vehicles: some snow plows have a wing that extends as far as three metres to the right of the vehicle. On freeways, several snow plows may be staggered across the road, clearing all lanes at the same time by passing a ridge of snow from plow to plow. Do not try to pass between them. This is extremely dangerous because there is not enough room to pass safely, and the ridge of wet snow can throw your vehicle out of control.

Chapter 3, section I — Summary
By the end of this section you should know:
- How to identify and manage situations where your visibility may be reduced
- How weather conditions such as rain, flooded roads, snow and ice may affect your vehicle and your ability to control it
- What to do if your vehicle skids or if you encounter heavy snow, whiteouts or black ice
- How to recognize and share the road with snow removal vehicles

---

II. Dealing with particular situations

Drowsy driving

Drowsiness has been identified as a causal factor in a growing number of collisions resulting in injury and fatality. Tired drivers can be as impaired as drunk drivers. They have a slower reaction time and are less alert.

Studies have shown that collisions involving drowsiness tend to occur during late night/early morning hours (between 2:00 am and 6:00 am) or late afternoon (between 2:00 pm and 4:00 pm). Studies also indicate that shift workers, people with undiagnosed or untreated sleep disorders, and commercial vehicle operators, are at greater risk for such collisions.

Always avoid driving when you are feeling drowsy. Scientific research confirms that you can fall asleep without actually being aware of it. Here are eight important warning signs that your drowsiness is serious enough to place you at risk:

- You have difficulty keeping your eyes open
- Your head keeps tilting forward despite your efforts to keep your eyes on the road
- Your mind keeps wandering and you can't seem to concentrate
- You yawn frequently
- You can't remember details about the last few kilometres you have travelled
- You are missing traffic lights and signals
- Your vehicle drifts into the next lane and you have to jerk it back into your lane
- You have drifted off the road and narrowly avoided a crash

If you have one of these symptoms, you may be in danger of falling asleep. Pull off the road and park your vehicle in a safe, secure place. Use well-lit rest

stops or truck stops on busy roads. Stimulants are never a substitute for sleep. Drinks containing caffeine can help you feel more alert, but if you are sleep deprived, the effects wear off quickly. The same is true of turning up the volume of your radio or CD player and opening the window. You cannot trick your body into staying awake; you need to sleep. Remember, the only safe driver is a well-rested, alert driver.

Workers on the road

Be extra careful when driving through construction zones and areas where people are working on or near the road.

When approaching a construction zone, slow down and obey all warning signs and people and/or devices who are directing traffic through the area. Municipalities can lower the speed limits in construction zones to increase safety for workers. Reduced speed limits come into effect

once signs are posted in the area. In the construction zone, drive carefully and adjust your speed and driving to suit the conditions. Obey posted speed limits, do not change lanes, be ready for sudden stops and watch for workers and construction vehicles on the road and give them more room to ensure everyone's safety.

Traffic control workers control vehicle traffic in work zones and prevent conflicts between construction activity and traffic. Whether you are driving during the day or at night, watch for traffic control people and follow their instructions.

Treat people working on roads with respect and be patient if traffic is delayed. Sometimes traffic in one direction must wait while vehicles from the other direction pass through a detour. If your lane is blocked and no one is directing traffic, yield to the driver coming from the opposite direction. When the way is clear, move slowly and carefully around the obstacle.

Recent changes to the Highway Traffic Act have resulted in doubled fines for speeding in a construction zone when workers are present. It is also an offence to disobey **STOP** or **SLOW** signs displayed by a traffic control person or firefighter.

Animals on the road

You may come upon farm animals or wild animals on the road, especially in farming areas and in the northern parts of the province. Animal crossing signs warn drivers where there is a known danger of moose, deer or cattle stepping onto the road, but animals may appear anywhere. Always be alert for animals and ready to react.

Look well ahead. At night, use your highbeams where possible. When you see an animal, brake or slow down if you can without risk to vehicles behind you. If there is no traffic and no danger of colliding with any other object, steer around the animal, staying in control of your vehicle.

In some areas of the province, horse-drawn carriages may use the road. Be prepared to share the road with them.

Cellular phones and CB radios

Cellular phones and CB radios can be important safety aids for drivers. Many people use their phones or radios to report crimes and collisions and for personal safety when they are lost or their vehicles break down. But using a cellular phone or CB radio while driving takes a driver's attention from the business of driving. Distracted drivers are more likely to make a driving error or to react too slowly.

As more and more people use cellular phones, it is important that they be used safely. You should use your cellular phone only when you are parked. If you are driving and your phone rings, let your cellular voice mail service take the call and listen to the message later when you are parked. If you must use a cellular phone when driving, use a hands-free microphone. Make sure your phone is easy to see and reach and that you know how to use it. Use voice-activated or speed dialing and never take notes while driving.

Currently, there is no law against using CB radios or cellular phones while driving, but you can be charged with dangerous or careless driving if you cause a collision while using a cellular phone. Careless driving is a serious offence. Police can charge you with careless driving if you do not pay full attention to your driving. If you are convicted of careless driving, you will get six demerit points, a fine up to $1,000 and/or six months in jail. In some cases, your licence may be suspended for up to two years.

Driver distractions

Driving is a job that requires your full attention every time you get behind the wheel. Any secondary activity will detract from your ability to drive properly and safely. You must reduce distractions and focus on your driving.

There are a number of possible driver distractions including:

- Using devices such as GPS systems, stereos, CD and DVD players, radios, cell phones, laptops, Personal Digital Assistants (PDAs), and MP3 players
- Reading maps, directions or other material
- Grooming (combing hair, putting on make-up or shaving)
- Eating or drinking
- Taking notes
- Talking with passengers
- Tending to children or pets
- Adjusting the controls in your vehicle (radio, CD player or climate control)

Commercial passenger vehicle and school bus drivers need to be aware of potential situations that may distract them from driving. Some distractions occur outside the bus, such as motor vehicle collisions, scenery or road construction.

Drivers can also be distracted by situations inside the vehicle. In particular, school bus drivers deal with specific distractions such as high levels of noise and activity inside the vehicle. If a driver has to take his or her eyes off the road in order to address a behavioural issue, there is a greater risk of collision.

Tips to reduce driver distractions

- Attend to personal grooming and plan your route before you leave.
- Identify and preset your vehicle's climate control, radio and CD player.
- Make it a habit to pull over and park to use your cell phone or have a passenger take the call or let it go to voice mail.
- Put reading material away if you are tempted to read.
- Do not engage in emotional or complex conversations. Stress can affect your driving performance.
- When you are hungry or thirsty, take a break from driving.

Remember to focus on your driving at all times. A split-second distraction behind the wheel can result in injury or even death.

Emergency Vehicles

Emergency vehicles include fire and police department vehicles, ambulances and public utility emergency vehicles.

Reacting to an approaching emergency vehicle

When you see red or red AND blue flashing lights or hear the bells or sirens of an emergency vehicle approaching from either direction, you must immediately slow down, move as far to the right side of the roadway as you can, and stop.

Diagram 3-1

Stay alert. When you see an approaching emergency vehicle with its lights or siren on, prepare to clear the way.

- React quickly but calmly. Don't slam on the brakes or pull over suddenly. Use your signals to alert other drivers you intend to pull over.
- Check your rear-view mirrors. Look in front and on both sides of your vehicle. Allow other vehicles to also pull over. Pull to the right and gradually come to a stop.
- Wait for the emergency vehicle to pass and watch for other emergency vehicles that may be responding to the same call. Check to make sure the way is clear and signal before merging back into traffic.
- Don't drive on or block the shoulder on freeways. Emergency vehicles will use the shoulder of the road if all lanes are blocked.

Never follow or try to outrun an emergency vehicle. It is illegal to follow within 150 metres of a fire vehicle or ambulance responding to a call in any lane going in the same direction.

Failing to pull over and stop for an approaching emergency vehicle can result in a conviction and a fine.

Note: Some fire fighters and volunteer medical responders may display a flashing green light when using their own vehicles to respond to a fire or medical emergency. Please yield the right-of-way to help them reach the emergency quickly and safely.

Take lights and sirens seriously. Clear the way! Pull to the right and stop. It's the law.

Approaching a stopped emergency vehicle with red or red AND blue flashing lights

When you see an emergency vehicle stopped with its red or red AND blue flashing lights in a lane or on the shoulder in you direction of travel, you must slow down and pass with caution. If the road has two or more lanes, you must move over into another lane to allow one lane clearance between your vehicle and the emergency vehicle, if it can be done safely. Failing to follow these rules can result in a conviction, demerit points on your driving record, a driver's licence suspension of up to two years and a fine of $400 to $2,000 for a first offence and $1,000 to $4,000 for a 'subsequent' offence (a 'subsequent' offence is when you are convicted again within five years). The court can order you to spend up to six months in jail, or you may have to pay a fine or do both.

Chapter 3, section II — Summary
By the end of this section you should know:
- How to recognize the signs and dangers of drowsy driving
- How to manoeuvre your vehicle through construction zones
- What to do if you encounter animals on the road
- Things that may distract you when driving and how to minimize those distractions
- What to do when you encounter an emergency vehicle

III. Dealing with emergencies

Stall or breakdown procedure

If the vehicle stalls or breaks down on the highway, quickly and calmly act to protect the passengers and other motorists.

- Stop as far off the roadway as possible.
- If the vehicle cannot be moved off the highway, instruct the passengers to remain on the bus.
- If you cannot find and repair the trouble, remain with the vehicle and ask a responsible person to find help.
- Set out appropriate flares, lamps, lanterns or portable reflectors as required by the Highway Traffic Act at a distance of approximately 30 metres (100 ft) in advance of the vehicle and 30 metres (100 ft) to the rear. They must be visible from 150 metres (500 ft) in each direction.

In a collision where someone is injured

St. John Ambulance recommends that all drivers carry a well-stocked first aid kit and know how to use it. School buses must be equipped with a first aid kit. Consider reading a book about first aid or taking a first aid course. It could mean the difference between life and death in a collision.

Every driver involved in a collision must stay at the scene or return to it immediately and give all possible assistance. If you are not personally involved in a collision, you should stop to offer help if police or other help has not arrived.

In a collision with injuries, possible fuel leaks or serious vehicle damage, stay calm and follow these steps:

1. Call for help or have someone else call. By law, you must report any collision to the police when there are injuries or damage

to vehicles or other property exceeding $1,000.

2. Turn off all engines and turn on emergency flashers. Set up warning signals or flares and have someone warn approaching drivers.

3. Do not let anyone smoke, light a match or put flares near any vehicle in case of a fuel leak. If any of the vehicles is on fire, get the people out and make sure everyone is well out of the way. If there is no danger of fire or explosion, leave injured people where they are until trained medical help arrives.

4. If you are trained in first aid, treat injuries in the order of urgency, within the level of your training. For example, clear the person's airway to restore breathing, give rescue breathing or stop bleeding by applying pressure with a clean cloth.

5. If you are not trained in first aid, use common sense. For example, people in collisions often go into shock. Cover the person with a jacket or blanket to reduce the effects of shock.

6. Stay with injured people until help arrives.

7. Disabled vehicles on the road may be a danger to you and other drivers. Do what you can to make sure everyone involved in a collision is kept safe.

In a collision where no one is injured

Follow these steps in a collision where there are no injuries:

1. If the vehicles are driveable, move them as far off the road as possible — this should not affect the police officer's investigation. This is especially important on busy or high speed roads where it may be dangerous to leave vehicles in the driving lanes. If you cannot move the vehicles off the road, set up warning signals or flares far enough away to give other traffic time to slow down or stop.

2. Call police (provincial or local, depending on where the collision takes place). By law, you must report any collision to the police where there are injuries or damage to vehicles or property exceeding $1,000.

3. Give all possible help to police or anyone whose vehicle has been damaged. This includes giving police your name and address, the name and address of the registered owner of the vehicle, the vehicle plate and permit number and the liability insurance card.

4. Get the names, addresses and phone numbers of all witnesses.

5. If damage is less than $1,000, you are still required by law to exchange information with anyone whose vehicle has been damaged. However, the collision does not have to be reported to the police.

6. Contact your insurance company as soon as possible if you intend to make a claim.

Fires

There are three common causes of vehicle fires:
1. Leaking fuel
2. Electrical shorts
3. Overheated brakes

All buses and school buses are required to carry an adequate fire extinguisher. Every driver should know how to use the fire extinguisher.

Remember in case of fire:
1. Remove passengers from the vehicle quickly and in an orderly manner.
2. Direct passengers to a safe place.

Chapter 3, section III — Summary
By the end of this section you should know:
- What to do in emergency situations when your vehicle stalls or breaks down
- The steps to take if you are involved in a collision with or without injuries

Traffic laws include the traffic signs and lights, pedestrian signals and pavement markings that tell drivers and other road users what they must do in certain situations. This chapter shows you what many of those signs, lights and markings look like and explains what they mean to drivers.

I. Signs

Traffic signs give you important information about the law, warn you about dangerous conditions and help you find your way. Signs use different symbols, colours and shapes for easy identification.

Here are some of the many signs you will see on Ontario roads:

 A stop sign is eight-sided and has a red background with white letters. It means you must come to a complete stop. Stop at the stop line if it is marked on the pavement. If there is no stop line, stop at the crosswalk. If there is no crosswalk, stop at the edge of the sidewalk. If there is no sidewalk, stop at the edge of the intersection. Wait until the way is clear before entering the intersection.

 A school zone sign is five-sided and has a blue background with white symbols. It warns that you are coming to a school zone. Slow down, drive with extra caution and watch for children.

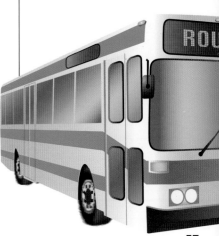

A yield sign is a triangle with a white background and a red border. It means you must let traffic in the intersection or close to it go first. Stop if necessary and go only when the way is clear.

A railway crossing sign is X-shaped with a white background and red outline. It warns that railway tracks cross the road. Watch for this sign. Slow down and look both ways for trains. Be prepared to stop.

There are four other kinds of signs: regulatory, warning, temporary conditions and information and direction.

Regulatory signs

These signs give a direction that must be obeyed. They are usually rectangular or square with a white or black background and black, white or coloured letters. A sign with a green circle means you may or must do the activity shown inside the ring. A red circle with a line through it means the activity shown is not allowed.

Here are some common regulatory signs:

This road is an official bicycle route. Watch for cyclists and be prepared to share the road with them.

You may park in the area between the signs during the times posted. (Used in pairs or groups.)

Snowmobiles may use this road.

Do not enter this road.

Do not stop in the area between the signs. This means you may not stop your vehicle in this area, even for a moment. (Used in pairs or groups.)

Do not stand in the area between the signs. This means you may not stop your vehicle in this area except while loading or unloading passengers. (Used in pairs or groups.)

Do not park in the area between the signs. This means you may not stop your vehicle except to load or unload passengers or merchandise. (Used in pairs or groups.)

Do not turn left at the intersection.

Do not drive through the intersection.

Do not turn to go in the opposite direction. (U-turn)

Do not turn right when facing a red light at the intersection.

Do not turn left during the times shown.

This parking space is only for vehicles displaying a valid Accessible Parking Permit.

No bicycles allowed on this road.

No pedestrians allowed on this road.

 Do not pass on this road.

   These signs, above the road or on the pavement before an intersection, tell drivers the direction they must travel. For example: the driver in lane one must turn left; the driver in lane two must turn left or go straight ahead; and the driver in lane three must turn right.

 Keep to the right of the traffic island.

Slow traffic on multi-lane roads must keep right.

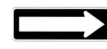 Traffic may travel in one direction only.

 Speed limit changes ahead.

 The speed limit in this zone is lower during school hours. Observe the speed limit shown when the yellow lights are flashing.

  This is a pedestrian crossover. Be prepared to stop and yield right-of-way to pedestrians.

This sign, above the road or on the ground, means the lane is only for two-way left turns.

This sign reserves curb area for vehicles displaying a valid Accessible Person Parking Permit picking up and dropping off passengers with disabilities.

These signs mean lanes are only for specific types of vehicles, either all the time or during certain hours. Different symbols are used for the different types of vehicles. They include: buses, taxis, vehicles with three or more people and bicycles.

Keep to the right lane except when passing on two-lane sections where climbing or passing lanes are provided.

High Occupancy Vehicle (HOV) signs

Only public vehicles such as buses, or passenger vehicles carrying a specified minimum number of passengers, may use this lane.

Vehicles cannot change lanes into or out of a high occupancy vehicle lane in this area.

STOP FOR
SCHOOL BUS
WHEN SIGNALS
FLASHING

Stop for school bus when signals are flashing.

STOP FOR
SCHOOL BUS
WHEN SIGNALS
FLASHING
BOTH DIRECTIONS

This sign is installed on multi-lane highways with no centre median divider. It informs drivers approaching from both directions that they must stop for a school bus when its signal lights are flashing.

No trucks in this lane.

No trucks in indicated lane.

No trucks over 6.5 metres in indicated lane.

No trucks over 6.5 metres in length in this lane.

Heavy trucks permitted on this roadway.

Road forks to the right.

No heavy trucks permitted on this roadway.

No heavy trucks permitted on this roadway between the hours of 7 p.m. – 7 a.m.

MAXIMUM WEIGHT 10 tonnes

No vehicles over 10 tonnes on this roadway.

LOAD RESTRICTION IN EFFECT 5 tonnes per axle

No vehicles that bear more than 5 tonnes per axle permitted on this roadway.

MAXIMUM WEIGHT
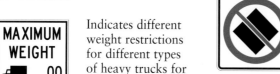 **00 00 00 tonnes**

Indicates different weight restrictions for different types of heavy trucks for a bridge structure.

DANGEROUS GOODS ROUTE

Trucks carrying dangerous materials permitted on this roadway.

Trucks carrying dangerous materials permitted on this roadway.

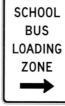

Trucks carrying dangerous materials are not permitted on this roadway.

DANGEROUS GOODS CARRIERS PROHIBITED

No vehicles containing hazardous materials permitted on this roadway.

SCHOOL BUS LOADING ZONE →

School bus loading zone, proceed with caution.

TRUCKS ENTER INSPECTION STATION WHEN LIGHTS FLASHING

Trucks must enter inspection station when signals are flashing.

(407) **ETR**
Express Toll Route
Vehicles Over 5 Tonnes
Must Have Valid Transponder

Any trucks over 5 tonnes must have a valid 407 transponder to use ETR.

Warning signs

These signs warn of dangerous or unusual conditions ahead such as a curve, turn, dip or sideroad. They are usually diamond-shaped and have a yellow background with black letters or symbols.

Here are some common warning signs:

USE LOWER GEAR

Trucks are advised to use a lower gear when travelling this portion of roadway.

ONE LANE ONLY WHEN USED BY TRUCKS

Indicates that horizontal clearance does not allow room for another vehicle when structure is being used by a truck.

3.9m

Maximum vertical clearance of 3.9 metres.

Maximum vertical clearance of 3.9 metres under this obstruction.

OVERHEIGHT

Indicates that an upcoming structure might not allow room for a tall truck, and should therefore choose an alternate route.

WHEN FLASHING

Tab indicates that sign has pertinence when lights are flashing.

Trucks are advised to slow down around this curve due to its smaller radius.

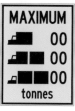

Trucks over 10 tonnes are advised not to use this roadway.

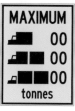

Advises trucks to use caution if they are over indicated weight restrictions for their truck type.

Indicates an upcoming truck entrance on the right and vehicles should be prepared to yield to trucks entering the roadway.

Indicates an upcoming truck entrance and vehicles should be prepared to yield to trucks entering the roadway.

Indicates an upcoming bus entrance on the right and vehicles should be prepared to yield to buses entering the roadway.

Indicates an upcoming fire truck entrance on the right and vehicles should be prepared to yield to trucks entering the roadway.

Indicates an upcoming fire truck entrance and vehicles should be prepared to yield to trucks entering the roadway.

School bus stop ahead, proceed with caution.

Narrow bridge ahead.

Pavement narrows ahead.

Chevron (arrowhead) signs are posted in groups to guide drivers around sharp curves in the road.

Road branching off ahead.

Slight bend or curve in the road ahead.

Winding road ahead.

Intersection ahead. The arrow shows which direction of traffic has the right-of-way.

Posted under a curve warning, this sign shows the maximum safe speed for the curve.

The bridge ahead lifts or swings to let boats pass.

Drivers on the sideroad at the intersection ahead don't have a clear view of traffic.

Sharp bend or turn in the road ahead.

Paved surface ends ahead.

Bicycle crossing ahead.

 Stop sign ahead. Slow down.

 Share the road with oncoming traffic.

 Pavement is slippery when wet. Slow down and drive with caution.

 Hazard close to the edge of the road. The downward lines show the side on which you may safely pass.

 The road ahead is split into two separate roads by a median. Keep to the right-hand road. Each road carries one-way traffic.

 Right lane ends ahead. If you are in the right-hand lane you must merge safely with traffic in the lane to the left.

 Traffic lights ahead. Slow down.

 Steep hill ahead. You may need to use a lower gear.

Two roads going in the same direction are about to join into one. Drivers on both roads are equally responsible for seeing that traffic merges smoothly and safely.

Snowmobiles cross this road.

Divided highway ends: traffic travels in both directions on the same road ahead. Keep to the right.

Underpass ahead. Take care if you are driving a tall vehicle. Sign shows how much room you have.

Bump or uneven pavement on the road ahead. Slow down and keep control of your vehicle.

Railway crossing ahead. Be alert for trains. This sign also shows the angle at which the railway tracks cross the road.

Sharp turn or bend in the road in the direction of the arrow. The checkerboard border warns of danger. Slow down; be careful.

Deer regularly cross this road; be alert for animals.

Truck entrance on the right side of the road ahead. If the sign shows the truck on the left, the entrance is on the left side of the road.

Shows maximum safe speed on ramp.

 Watch for pedestrians and be prepared to share the road with them.

Watch for fallen rock and be prepared to avoid a collision.

 There may be water flowing over the road.

 This sign warns you that you are coming to a hidden school bus stop. Slow down, drive with extra caution, watch for children and for a school bus with flashing red lights.

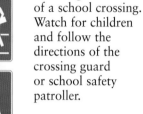 These signs warn of a school crossing. Watch for children and follow the directions of the crossing guard or school safety patroller.

Temporary condition signs

These signs warn of unusual temporary conditions such as road work zones, diversions, detours, lane closures or traffic control people on the road. They are usually diamond-shaped with an orange background and black letters or symbols.

Here are some common temporary condition signs:

Road work ahead.

You are entering a construction zone. Drive with extra caution and be prepared for a lower speed limit.

Survey crew working on the road ahead.

Temporary detour from normal traffic route.

Construction work one kilometre ahead.

Traffic control person ahead. Drive slowly and watch for instructions.

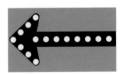

Flashing lights on the arrows show the direction to follow.

Pavement has been milled or grooved. Your vehicle's stopping ability may be affected so obey the speed limit and drive with extra caution. Motorcyclists may experience reduced traction on these surfaces.

Closed lane. Adjust speed to merge with traffic in lane indicated by arrow.

Reduce speed and be prepared to stop.

Do not pass the pilot or pace vehicle bearing this sign.

Follow detour marker until you return to regular route.

Lane ahead is closed for roadwork. Obey the speed limit and merge with traffic in the open lane.

Information and direction signs

These signs tell you about distances and destinations. They are usually rectangular with a green background and white letters. Other signs with different colours guide you to facilities, services and attractions.

Here are some common information and direction signs:

 Shows directions to nearby towns and cities.

 Shows the distances in kilometres to towns and cities on the road.

 Various exit signs are used on freeways. In urban areas, many exit ramps have more than one lane. Overhead and ground-mounted signs help drivers choose the correct lane to exit or stay on the freeway.

 Advance signs use arrows to show which lanes lead off the freeway. Signs are also posted at the exit.

 Sometimes one or more lanes may lead off the freeway. The arrows matching the exit lanes are shown on the advance sign in a yellow box with the word 'exit' under them.

 Freeway interchanges or exits have numbers that correspond to the distance from the beginning of the freeway. For example, interchange number 204 on Highway 401 is 204 kilometres from Windsor, where the freeway begins. Distances can be calculated by subtracting one interchange number from another.

The term 'VIA' is used to describe the roads that must be followed to reach a destination.

These signs change according to traffic conditions to give drivers current information on delays and lane closures ahead.

Shows off-road facilities such as hospitals, airports, universities or carpool lots.

Shows route to passenger railway station.

Shows route to airport.

Shows route to ferry service.

Shows facilities that are accessible by wheelchair.

Other signs

Here are some other common signs:

The slow-moving vehicle sign is orange with a red border. Motor vehicles moving slower than 40 km/h must have this sign on the rearmost part of the vehicle when it is being driven on a road, unless they are only crossing it. The sign cannot be used on any other vehicle or object. It alerts other drivers that the vehicle ahead of them is traveling at a much slower speed than the general flow of traffic. The slow-moving vehicle sign is predominately used by farmers on farm machinery driven on public roads.

II. Traffic lights

Emergency response signs

Some information signs include a numbering system along the bottom of the sign to assist emergency vehicles in determining an appropriate route.

Bilingual signs

Watch for these signs when driving in designated bilingual areas. Read the messages in the language you understand best. Bilingual messages may be together on the same sign or separate, with an English sign immediately followed by a French sign.

Traffic lights tell drivers and pedestrians what they must do at intersections and along roads. They tell road users when to stop and go, when and how to turn and when to drive with extra caution.

Green light

A green light means you may turn left, go straight or turn right after yielding to vehicles and pedestrians already in the intersection. When turning left or right you must yield the right-of-way to pedestrians crossing the intersection.

Yellow light

A yellow — or amber — light means the red light is about to appear. You must stop if you can do so safely; otherwise, go with caution.

Red light

A red light means you must stop. Bring your vehicle to a complete stop at the stop line if it is marked on the pavement. If there is no stop line, stop at the crosswalk, marked or not. If there is no crosswalk, stop at the edge of the sidewalk. If there is no sidewalk, stop at the edge of the intersection.

Wait until the light changes to green and the intersection is clear before moving through it.

Unless a sign tells you not to, you may turn right on a red light only after coming to a complete stop and waiting until the way is clear. You may also turn left on a red light if you are moving from a one-way road onto a one-way road, but you must come to a complete stop first and wait until the way is clear.

Lights and arrows to help turning vehicles

Flashing green lights and green arrows direct drivers who are turning.

Advance green light or arrow

When you face a flashing green light or a left-pointing green arrow and a green light, you

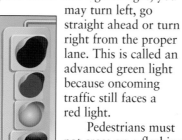

may turn left, go straight ahead or turn right from the proper lane. This is called an advanced green light because oncoming traffic still faces a red light.

Pedestrians must not cross on a flashing green light unless a pedestrian signal tells them to.

Simultaneous left turn

When a left-turn green arrow is shown with a red light, you may turn left from the left-turn lane. Vehicles turning left from the opposite direction may also be making left turns because they too face a left-turn green arrow.

After the left-turn green arrow, a yellow arrow may appear. This means the green light is about to appear for traffic in one or both directions. Do not start your left turn. Stop if you can do so safely; otherwise, complete your turn with caution.

You can still turn left when the light is green, but only when the way is clear of traffic and pedestrians. If the light turns red when you are in the intersection, complete your turn when it is safe.

Pedestrians must not cross on a left-turn green arrow unless a pedestrian signal tells them to.

Transit Priority Signals

Traffic and pedestrians must yield to public transit vehicles at a transit priority signal. The round signal is on top of a regular traffic signal and shows a white vertical bar on a dark background. This allows transit vehicles to go through, turn right or left, while all conflicting traffic faces a red light.

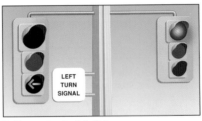

Fully protected left turn

Some intersections have separate traffic lights for left-turning traffic and for traffic going through the intersection or turning right.

When a left-turn green arrow appears for traffic in the left-turn lane, traffic going straight ahead or turning right will usually see a red light. You may turn left from the left-turn lane when you face a green arrow. Vehicles from the opposite direction may also be turning left.

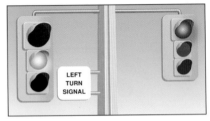

After the left-turn green arrow, a yellow light appears for left-turning vehicles only.

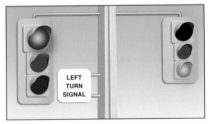

After the yellow light, a red light appears for left-turning vehicles only. Traffic going straight ahead or turning right will face a green light or green arrows pointing straight ahead and to the right.

In these intersections, you may not begin turning left after the green light appears for traffic going straight ahead or turning right. If the light turns yellow while you are in the intersection, complete your turn with caution.

Flashing red light

You must come to a complete stop at a flashing red light. Move through the intersection only when it is safe.

Flashing yellow light

A flashing yellow light means you should drive with caution when approaching and moving through the intersection.

Blank traffic lights

During an electrical power loss, traffic lights at intersections will not work. Yield the right-of-way to vehicles in the intersection and to vehicles entering the intersection from your right. Go cautiously and use the intersection the same way you would use an intersection with all-way stop signs.

Traffic beacons

A traffic beacon is a single flashing light hung over an intersection or placed over signs or on obstacles in the road.

Flashing red beacon

A flashing red beacon above an intersection or stop sign means you must come to a complete stop. Move through the intersection only when it is safe to do so.

Flashing yellow beacon

A flashing yellow beacon above an intersection, above a warning sign or on an obstruction in the road, warns you to drive with caution.

III. Pedestrian signals

Pedestrian signals help pedestrians cross at intersections with traffic lights. The signal for pedestrians to walk is a white walking symbol. A flashing or steady orange hand symbol means pedestrians must not begin to cross.

A pedestrian facing a walk signal may cross the road in the direction of the signal. While crossing, pedestrians have the right-of-way over all vehicles.

A pedestrian facing a flashing or steady hand symbol should not begin to cross the road. Pedestrians who have already begun to cross when the hand signal appears should go as quickly as possible to a safe area. While they are crossing, pedestrians still have the right-of-way over vehicles.

At intersections with traffic lights where there are no pedestrian signals, pedestrians facing a green light may cross. Pedestrians may not cross on a flashing green light or a left-turn green arrow.

Intersection pedestrian signals

On a busy main road, an intersection pedestrian signal helps people to cross the road safely by signalling traffic to stop. The intersection pedestrian signal has one or more crosswalks, pedestrian walk and don't walk signals, push buttons for pedestrians, and traffic signal lights on the main road only.

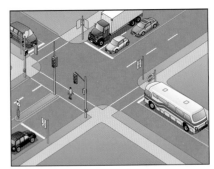

Stop signs control traffic on the smaller, less busy crossroad.

You must observe, obey the traffic rules, and use your safe driving skills to drive through these intersections. (See Yielding the right-of-way on page 35.)

IV. Pavement markings

Pavement markings work with road signs and traffic lights to give you important information about the direction of traffic and where you may and may not travel. Pavement markings divide traffic lanes, show turning lanes, mark pedestrian crossings, indicate obstacles, and tell you when it is not safe to pass.

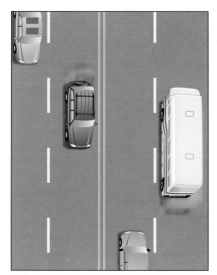

Diagram 4-1
Yellow lines separate traffic travelling in opposite directions. White lines separate traffic travelling in the same direction.

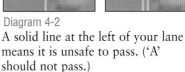

Diagram 4-2
A solid line at the left of your lane means it is unsafe to pass. ('A' should not pass.)

Diagram 4-3

A broken line at the left of your lane means you may pass if the way is clear. ('A' may pass if there are enough broken lines ahead to complete the pass safely.)

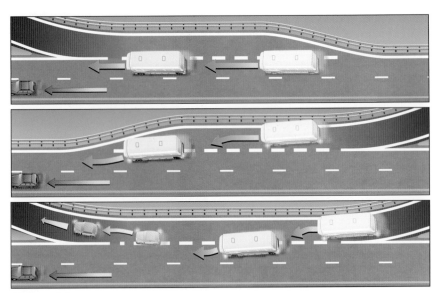

Diagram 4-4

Broken lines that are wider and closer together than regular broken lines are called continuity lines. When you see continuity lines on your left side, it generally means the lane you are in is ending or exiting and that you must change lanes if you want to continue in your current direction. Continuity lines that appear only on your right mean your lane will continue unaffected.

Diagram 4-5

A stop line is a single white line painted across the road at an intersection. It shows where you must stop. If there is no stop line marked on the road, stop at the crosswalk, marked or not. If there is no crosswalk, stop at the edge of the sidewalk. If there is no sidewalk, stop at the edge of the intersection.

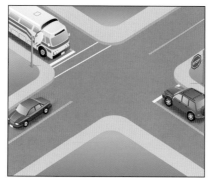

Diagram 4-6

A crosswalk is marked by two parallel white lines painted across the road. However, crosswalks at intersections are not always marked. If there is no stop line, stop at the crosswalk, marked or not. If there is no crosswalk, stop at the edge of the sidewalk. If there is no sidewalk, stop at the edge of the intersection.

Diagram 4-7

A white arrow painted on a lane means you may move only in the direction of the arrow.

Diagram 4-8

A pedestrian crossing — or crossover — is marked by two white double parallel lines across the road with an X in each lane approaching it. Stop before the line and yield to pedestrians.

Diagram 4-9

Two solid lines painted on the pavement guide traffic away from fixed objects such as bridge piers or concrete islands. Usually a sign is affixed to the object, and the object is painted with yellow and black markings.

Chapter 4 — Summary

By the end of this chapter you should know:

Signs

- The difference between regulatory, warning, temporary condition and information/ direction signs
- How to read the symbols and messages of some common signs in each category

Traffic Lights

- The different colours and symbols that appear on traffic lights and what those mean
- How to navigate turns using advanced green lights and arrows
- How to proceed when approaching flashing amber or red lights
- What to do in situations where the traffic lights are not operating

Pedestrian Signals

- What the symbols on pedestrian signals indicate
- What an intersection pedestrian signal is and what to do if you encounter one

Pavement Markings

- How pavement markings are used to control traffic
- What the different colours and types of markings are used to indicate

Chapter 5

I. Loading and unloading passengers

As a school bus driver, it is your responsibility to ensure the safety of your passengers. This is especially important to remember when you are loading or unloading your passengers, as these are the times at which they are most vulnerable.

"Spotters" or safety patrollers may help the school bus driver when loading or unloading a school bus. The spotter can prevent the driver from hitting children who may have stopped in a blind area in front of the vehicle.

Recently developed safety equipment includes newly designed mirrors or multiple mirror adjustment systems, motion detector systems, bumper-mounted crossing barriers, and perimeter braking systems. When drivers and passengers are trained to use them effectively, they will enhance safety.

Keep the following rules in mind:
- Turn on the upper alternating red signal lights before stopping to load or unload your passengers.
- As soon as the bus is stopped, extend the Stop Arm and the Pedestrian Student Safety Crossing Arm.
- Remain stopped with the lights flashing and the stop and crossing arms extended until all passengers who must cross the highway have completed the crossing.
- Do not load or unload passengers on a steep grade or curve. You should have a clear view of the road in each direction for at least 150 m (500 ft).
- Stop on the travelled portion of the roadway and not the shoulder to load or unload passengers.

85

- Never load the bus beyond its licensed capacity.

Loading or unloading passengers at traffic signal lights

When loading or unloading at traffic signal lights, **do not** activate the upper alternating red flashing lights and stop arm on the school bus. The stop should be made as close as possible to the intersection, close to the curb or edge of the roadway and the passengers cautioned to obey the traffic signal lights.

If a driver needs to stop near an intersection with traffic signal lights and use the flashing red lights and stop arm, the stop should be made at least 60 m from the intersection.

School bus loading zones

School bus loading zones are areas of a roadway or school driveway designated as passenger loading/unloading zones by signs that set out the limits of the zones.

In school bus loading zones, stop the school bus close to the right curb or edge of the roadway between the signs setting out the limits of the zone.

Keep in mind these two important rules of school bus loading zones:

1. **Do not** operate the flashing lights and stop arm within a school bus loading zone.
2. **Do not** stop your bus to load or unload passengers on the opposite side of the highway from a school bus loading zone.

Rules for passengers

As the driver, you must ensure that your passengers observe the following rules:

- Upon entering the bus, passengers should go directly to their seats and sit down. All passengers should be seated before you move the bus again.
- Passengers should not enter or leave the bus while it is moving.

- Passengers should not obstruct the vision of the driver to the front, sides or rear.
- Passengers should stay seated until the bus has come to a full stop.
- Passengers leaving the vehicle should cross only in front of the bus and approximately three metres (10 ft) from the front of the bus, using the safety crossing arm as a guide.
- When more than one student leaves the bus, students should form a group approximately three metres (10 ft) (the length of the safety crossing arm) from the front of the bus and on the right shoulder or curb of the road; the group should then look for the driver's signal indicating it is safe to cross.
- Passengers who remain on the right side of the stopped bus should form a group and stay together, away from the front

right corner of the bus, until the bus moves away.

- Passengers should look both ways before stepping into the roadway and continue to watch for traffic, as they cross.
- Passengers should always cross the roadway at a right angle to the bus, never diagonally.
- Passengers should walk, never run, when crossing the roadway.

Note: Before driving off, you should check the convex cross-over mirrors to ensure that no passengers are crossing in front of the school bus.

II. Special safety precautions for school bus drivers

- When the bus is moving, the doors should be safely closed, but must not be locked.
- Do not allow passengers to obstruct your vision to the front, sides or rear.
- Never permit an unauthorized person to sit in the driver's seat, operate the vehicle, or any of its controls.
- No lunch pails, books or parcels should be in the aisles or step wells, at any time.
- Never leave the vehicle without first stopping the engine, setting the brakes, putting the transmission on its lowest gear or park position and removing the ignition key. Some automatic transmission vehicles do not have a 'park' position. If this is the case the vehicle should be parked

with the transmission in 'neutral' and the parking brake set.
- When a school bus is disabled on a roadway when lights are required, flares or reflectors must be placed 30 m (100 ft) in front and behind the vehicle.

Reversing a school bus

Use care and caution when you are backing a school bus. Use the rear view mirror, turn and look back and have someone give directions. Back slowly and cautiously, and watch traffic conditions around the vehicle at all times. Drivers should not back up their vehicles on school grounds or at loading or unloading stops or zones without proper guidance and signals from a responsible person outside the bus.

Stopping at railway crossings

School buses must stop at least five metres (16.5 ft) from the nearest rail at all railway crossings. While stopped, the driver must open the bus door and look and listen for any approaching trains. The driver must not change gears when the bus is actually crossing the tracks. The flashing lights and stop arm must not be activated in this situation.

When stopped for a period of time waiting at an intersection or railway crossing, it is a safe practice to place the gear shift lever in neutral and release the clutch. Always set the parking brake.

III. Stopping for school buses law

Stopping requirements

The stopping for school buses law applies everywhere, regardless of the posted speed limit — on highways, county roads, city, town or village streets.

Motorists meeting (approaching from the opposite direction) a stopped school bus with its overhead red signal lights flashing, must stop before reaching the bus and shall not proceed until the bus moves or the overhead lights have stopped flashing. The only exception is on highways divided by a median; drivers on the other side of the median approaching from the opposite are not required to stop. (A median is a raised, lowered or earth strip dividing a road where vehicles travel in both directions.)

Diagram 5-1

Motorists approaching a stopped school bus from the rear with its overhead red signals lights flashing, shall stop at least 20 metres before reaching the bus and shall not proceed until the bus moves, or the overhead lights have stopped flashing.

Drivers who don't stop for a school bus can be fined $400 to $2,000 and get six demerit points for a first offence. If you break the rule a second time within five years, the penalty is a fine of $1,000 to $4,000 and six demerit points. You could also go to jail for up to six months.

If the driver is not charged, the vehicle's registered owner can be fined $400 to $2,000 for a first offence and $1,000 to $4,000 for subsequent offences within a five-year period if their vehicle illegally passes a school bus that is stopped with its red lights flashing. If the vehicle owner does not pay the fine, they will not be able to renew the vehicle's permit.

Stopping for school bus law does not apply to all school-purposes buses

The school bus stopping law only applies to chrome yellow school buses with proper markings and signals as defined in Section 175 of the Highway Traffic Act and only when loading or unloading adults with developmental handicaps or children. Drivers of other school purposes vehicles must remember that they do not have the protection of this law and be very careful when choosing places to stop and directing their passengers as they leave the bus.

Reporting a school bus being passed

In Ontario, school bus drivers and other witnesses can report vehicles

Diagram 5-2

that have illegally passed a school bus. The **Illegal Passing of a School Bus Reporting Form** is available at the MTO website **www.mto.gov.on.ca**. This reporting form must be completed in its entirety before police action can be taken. You may also go to a police station to make a report. You may be required at a later date to attend court to provide evidence of what happened. A copy of the completed form may also be provided to a person charged with an offence so that he or she has a summary of what you will say in court. **The completed form should be delivered to your local police station as soon after the incident as possible.**

IV. Emergency evacuation of school buses

It is important that you and your passengers know how to get out of the bus using the emergency exits, and how to use the safety equipment.

It is your responsibility to set up routine evacuation practice. In an emergency, practice can mean an orderly and speedy evacuation even if you are injured and unable to help. This practice should take place at the beginning of the school year and every month afterwards.

Coordinate practice drills with the school administration and hold your drills in a safe, traffic-free area on school property.

The objective is to get the children off the bus safely in the shortest possible time and in an orderly way.

Here are three standard ways to evacuate a school bus:
- Through the front exit only
- Through the rear exit only
- Through the front and rear exits simultaneously

School buses manufactured on or after June 01, 2000, are fitted with a roof hatch as an alternative means of escape. The roof hatch, if fitted, and the push out windows can be used for exiting in an emergency situation.

Evacuation procedure

1. Assess the situation. Generally, the quickest method is to use both front and rear doors. If those exits expose people to other dangers such as fire or traffic, choose the safest exit.
2. Remain calm. Speak loudly, but slowly. Ask the passengers to move calmly to the exit you choose.
3. Assign a responsible leader to count the passengers as they leave and lead them to a safe area away from the bus. The leader should keep everyone together.
4. Assign some taller students to wait at the rear exit on the ground at either side of the door to help as the students swing

down. Another student inside tells the exiting person to "watch your head, put your hands on the helper's shoulders and swing down".

5. While the other students remain in their seats, the students closest to danger should leave one seat at a time by walking to the exit.

6. All articles such as lunches, books, and so on, should be left behind.

7. As the last person leaves, walk the length of the bus to be sure everyone is out and then exit yourself. Begin first aid treatment if necessary. Assign two responsible students to go for help if needed and organize helpers to put out warning flares or reflectors as required.

Practice cannot eliminate all injury, but it will certainly reduce the possibility of unnecessary injury to yourself, your passengers and other motorists.

V. Care and maintenance of a school bus

Mechanical fitness of school purposes vehicles

Regulations under the Highway Traffic Act require regular inspection of every station wagon, van, or bus operated by or under contract to a school board or other authority in charge of a school for the transportation of:

a) six or more adults with a developmental handicap,

b) six or more children, or

c) six or more persons referred to in a and b, between their homes and schools.

Inspections are also required for a chrome yellow school bus transporting children between their homes and churches or adults with a developmental handicap between their homes and training centres.

These vehicles must display valid inspection sticker(s).

The inspection must be carried out in a licensed motor vehicle inspection station. Authorized inspection mechanics perform the inspection and affix stickers to vehicles found to be satisfactory.

School buses are subject to random safety inspections by Ministry of Transportation staff throughout the year.

A clean school bus

The driver should keep the vehicle clean. Passengers will take pride in a bus that is neat and clean, and will cooperate in keeping it that way.

Daily cleaning routine

The floor should be swept, seats dusted and inspected for damage and breakage. The side windows, windshield and mirrors should be cleaned, along with lights and reflectors.

Weekly cleaning routine

Floors and seats should be washed. The exterior should be washed and the paint inspected. Door hinges and operating mechanisms should be oiled and checked.

VI. School bus routes

The owner and driver of a school bus should be thoroughly familiar with the area. When route layouts are considered, the driver should help make recommendations to the school board, parents and where applicable, the vehicle owner. A well planned route can be the safest. Information on the route should be available to everyone affected by the service.

Consider these factors when laying out routes and planning schedules:

- Age, health and physical condition of the passengers
- Condition of the roads to be travelled
- School schedule
- Distances between homes and school
- Distances between homes and routes
- Safety of walking routes between homes and routes
- Number and size of available buses
- Number of passengers to be served
- Size of area
- Location of bus stops
- Seasonal conditions (such as snow banks.)
- Location of safe turn-around points

In choosing a route:

- Examine bad curves, steep hills, rough roads, narrow bridges, railroad crossings and other hazards. Avoid these hazards whenever possible.
- Make sure bus stops are free from physical hazards.
- Route buses as near to the homes of passengers as traffic, time and convenience permit.
- Where possible, pick up and drop off passengers on the home side of the road, to eliminate or reduce the number of passengers forced to cross the road.
- Prepare and follow a time schedule.

- Make sure turn-around points are safe in all weather, with firm traction and good visibility of oncoming traffic.

Chapter 5 — Summary

By the end of this chapter you should know:

- How to load and unload passengers
- The stopping for school buses law and to whom it applies
- Special precautions for school buses
- Emergency procedures and evacuation process
- School bus daily care and maintenance
- Planning and designing a school bus route

Chapter 6

KEEPING YOUR LICENCE

Ontario has a one-piece driver's licence. The licence card has a photograph and signature of the driver. All drivers in Ontario should have a one-piece licence card. You must carry your licence with you whenever you drive.

Renewing your licence

When your licence is due for renewal, you will get a renewal application form in the mail. Most class B, C, E and F drivers are required to pass a vision and a written test at the time of the renewal. Drivers with class A, B, C, E or F licences who are 65 or older, must pass a vision, written and road test every year. If any tests are required, you must complete the tests at a DriveTest Centre prior to renewal. If no tests are required, you must renew your licence in person at a Driver and Vehicle Licence Issuing Office.

Take the form into any Driver and Vehicle Licence Issuing Office in the province. They are all equipped to take photographs. You will be asked to sign the form, show identification, pay a fee and have your photograph taken. You will get a temporary licence on the spot if your application and documents are in order, and your permanent one will be mailed to you. You must carry it with you whenever you drive and produce it when a police officer requests it.

If you do not get a renewal application form in the mail when your licence is due for renewal, call the Ministry of Transportation. You are responsible for making sure you have a valid driver's licence.

If your licence has been suspended, cancelled or expired for more than three years, you will

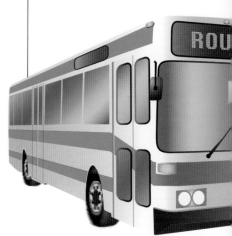

be required to reapply for a licence in Ontario and meet all the requirements of graduated licensing, including passing all the required tests. Only then will you be eligible to reapply for any commercial class licences.

Medical reporting

If you have any commercial vehicle driver's licence other than a class D licence, you must pass a medical examination every three to five years, depending on your age. You will get a notice and a blank medical report form in the mail three months before your medical report is due. You must go to a doctor and get a medical examination. The doctor completes the form. You must submit the form to the Ministry of Transportation, either by mail or in person. If you do not file a medical report, your class of licence will be downgraded.

- Drivers under the age of 46 are required to submit a medical report every five years.

- Drivers aged 46 to 64 are required to submit a medical report every three years.
- Drivers aged 65 or older are required to submit a medical report every year.

Changing your name or address

You must tell the Ministry of Transportation within six days of changing your name or address.

You will need a new licence when you change your address. You can change your address on the ServiceOntario website at www.serviceontario.ca, or at a Driver and Vehicle Licence Issuing Office, or mail it to the Ministry of Transportation, P.O. Box 9200, Kingston, ON, K7L 5K4. The ministry will send you a new licence.

Reason For Name Change	Documentation Required
Marriage	Government Issued Marriage Certificate Change of Name Certificate
Common Law Alliance	Change of Name Certificate
Adoption	Court Order for Adoption Change of Name Certificate
Under the Change of Name Act	Change of Name Certificate

When you get it, destroy your old licence and carry the new one.

If you change your name, you need a new licence. Take the documents you must show and your current licence to a Driver and Vehicle Licence Issuing Office. A new photograph will be taken. You will get a temporary licence to use until your permanent licence is mailed to you. Carry it with you whenever you drive.

There is no charge for getting a new licence because you change your name or address.

The chart on the previous page shows the documents you will need to change your name on your driver's licence.

Driver's licence laws

It is illegal to:
- Lend your licence
- Let someone else use it
- Use an altered licence
- Use another licence as your own
- Have more than one Ontario driver's licence
- Use a fictitious or imitation licence

The demerit point system

The demerit point system encourages drivers to improve their behaviour and protects people from drivers who abuse the privilege of driving. Drivers convicted of driving-related offences have demerit points recorded on their records. Demerit points stay on your record for two years from the date of the offence. If you accumulate too many demerit points, your driver's licence can be suspended.

Fully licensed drivers — Demerit Point System for Fully Licensed Drivers

6 points
You will be told about your record and urged to improve your driving skills

9 or more points
You may have to go to an interview to discuss your record and give reasons why your licence should

Table of offences

not be suspended. You may also have to complete a driver re-examination. If you fail this test, your licence can be cancelled. If you fail to attend an interview, or fail to give good reasons for keeping your licence, your licence may be suspended.

15 points

Your licence will be suspended for 30 days from the date you hand over your licence to the Ministry of Transportation. You can lose your licence for up to two years if you fail to surrender it.

After the suspension, the number of points on your driver's record will be reduced to seven. Any extra points could again bring you to the interview level. If you reach 15 points again, your licence will be suspended for six months.

Note: Class B and E licence holders may have no more than eight demerit points.

Here are the demerit points for driving offences.

7 points
- Failing to remain at the scene of a collision
- Failing to stop for police

6 points
- Careless driving
- Racing
- Exceeding the speed limit by 50 km/h or more
- Failing to stop for a school bus

5 points
- Driver of bus failing to stop at unprotected railway crossing

4 points
- Exceeding the speed limit by 30 to 49 km/h
- Following too closely

3 points
- Exceeding the speed limit by 16 to 29 km/h
- Driving through, around or under a railway crossing barrier
- Failing to yield the right-of-way
- Failing to obey a stop sign, traffic light or railway crossing signal
- Failing to obey traffic control stop sign
- Failing to obey traffic control slow sign
- Failing to obey school crossing stop sign
- Failing to obey the directions of a police officer
- Driving the wrong way on a divided road
- Failing to report a collision to a police officer
- Improper driving where road is divided into lanes
- Crowding the driver's seat

- Going the wrong way on a one-way road
- Driving or operating a vehicle on a closed road
- Crossing a divided road where no proper crossing is provided
- Failing to slow and carefully pass a stopped emergency vehicle
- Failing to stop at a pedestrian crossing
- Failing to move, where possible, into another lane when passing a stopped emergency vehicle
- Driving a vehicle that is equipped with or carrying a speed measuring warning device (such as a radar detector)
- Improper use of a high occupancy vehicle (HOV) lane

2 points
- Failing to lower headlight beam
- Improper opening of a vehicle door
- Prohibited turns

- Towing people — on toboggans, bicycles, skis, for example
- Failing to obey signs
- Failing to share the road
- Improper right turn
- Improper left turn
- Failing to signal
- Unnecessary slow driving
- Reversing on a highway
- Driver failing to wear a seatbelt
- Driver failing to ensure infant passenger is secured
- Driver failing to ensure toddler passenger is secured
- Driver failing to ensure child is secured
- Driver failing to ensure passenger under 16 years is wearing seatbelt*
- Driver failing to ensure passenger under 16 years is occupying a position with a seatbelt*

* Does not apply when driving a bus not equipped with seatbelts

Other ways to lose your licence

Your licence may also be suspended for the following reasons:

Medical suspension

By law, all doctors must report the names and addresses of everyone 16 years or older who has a condition that may affect their ability to drive safely. For example, an addiction to alcohol or drugs is a condition that affects your ability to drive. Doctors report this information to the Ministry of Transportation and it is not given to anyone else. Your driver's licence may be suspended until new medical evidence shows that the condition does not pose a safety risk.

Discretionary HTA suspensions

Your licence may be suspended by court order following conviction for the following:
- If you don't tell the truth in an application, declaration, affidavit or paper required by the Highway

Traffic Act, its Regulations or the Ministry of Transportation
- If you don't tell the truth about vehicle liability insurance
- If you fail to insure your vehicle
- If you are convicted of some driving offences, included careless driving and driving 50 km/h or more over the speed limit
- If you repeatedly travel at 50km/h or more over the speed limit Drivers can be suspended for up to 30 days for a first offence, up to 60 days for a second offence, and up to one year for a third or subsequent offence within a five-year period

Mandatory HTA suspensions

Your licence **will** be suspended:
- If you are convicted of failing to stop for a police officer and the court believes you wilfully avoided police during pursuit — that you tried to escape the police (This is a Criminal Code offence.

Your licence will be suspended for a minimum of five years.)
- If you don't pay a traffic fine when ordered by the court

Administrative driver's licence suspension (ADLS)

Your licence will be suspended **immediately** for 90 days:
- If you fail or refuse to give a breath or blood sample when asked by police
- If your blood alcohol concentration is more than 80 milligrams in 100 millilitres of blood (.08)

This suspension takes effect while you are still at the roadside or at the police station. It is an administrative suspension by the Registrar of Motor Vehicles and is separate from any criminal charges or prosecution which may also take place. A $150 administrative monetary penalty is also imposed on driver's who receive an ADLS.

"Warn Range" suspension

Drivers who blow in the warn range of .05 to .08 pose an immediate danger to themselves and other road users. If caught driving in the warn range, you will receive an **immediate** driver's licence suspension at the roadside.
- for 3 days for a first occurrence.
- for 7 days for a second occurrence and you must undergo a remedial alcohol education program.
- for 30 days for a third or subsequent occurrence in a five-year period and you must undergo a remedial alcohol treatment program and have an ignition interlock condition placed on your licence for 6 months. If you choose not to install an ignition interlock device, you must not drive until the condition is removed from your licence.

A $150 administrative monetary penalty is also imposed on drivers suspended for registering in the warn range.

Your licence will be cancelled:

- If you fail a driver's re-examination
- If you don't pay your reinstatement fee or administrative monetary penalty
- If your cheque for licence fees is not honoured by your bank
- If you voluntarily surrender your driver's licence to the Ministry of Transportation or it is surrendered or returned by another jurisdiction

Criminal Code suspensions

You will receive a one-year licence suspension the first time you are convicted of a Criminal Code offence. If you are convicted of a second Criminal Code offence, your licence will be suspended for three years. A third Criminal Code offence will get you a lifetime suspension from driving with the possibility of reinstatement

after 10 years. Fourth time offenders convicted of a Criminal Code offence are suspended from driving for life with no possibility of reinstatement. Convictions will remain on your driver's record for a minimum of 10 years. The court may order that the mandatory period of a suspension for a Criminal Code offence be extended.

Your licence will be suspended if you are convicted of any of the following Criminal Code offences:

- Driving or having care and control of a vehicle while your ability is impaired by alcohol or drugs
- Refusing to submit to a breath test for alcohol
- Failing or refusing to provide a breath sample for roadside testing
- Driving or having care and control of a vehicle when your blood alcohol concentration is more than 80 milligrams per 100 millilitres of blood (.08)
- Driving or having care and control of a boat, motorized or not, when

your blood alcohol concentration is more than 80 milligrams per 100 millilitres of blood (.08)
- Failing to remain at the scene of a collision to escape criminal or civil liability
- Dangerous driving
- Causing bodily harm by criminal negligence
- Causing death by criminal negligence
- Failing to stop for police

Remedial measures

There are several types of remedial measures. The mandatory Back on Track program is for all drivers convicted of impaired driving-related Criminal Code offences. For drivers who repeatedly blow in the warn range of .05 to .08, there is a mandatory alcohol education for a second suspension which must be completed within 120 days of the suspension or an alcohol treatment program for a third or subsequent suspension which must be completed within 180 days of the suspension. A Driver Improvement interview is required for drivers convicted of non-impaired driving-related Criminal Code offences. If your driver's licence has been suspended because of a Criminal Code conviction, your licence will remain suspended until you have completed the remedial requirements.

Driving under suspension

You may not drive, under any circumstances, when your licence is suspended. If you are convicted of driving while your licence is suspended for an HTA offence, you will have to pay a fine of $1,000 to $5,000 for a first offence and $2,000 to $5,000 for a 'subsequent' offence. (A 'subsequent' offence is when you are convicted again within five years.) The court can order you to spend up to six months in jail, or you may have to pay a fine or do both. Six months will be

added to your current suspension as well.

If you are found guilty of driving while your licence is suspended for a Criminal Code offence, you face a fine of $5,000 to $25,000 for a first offence and $10,000 to $50,000 for a subsequent offence within five years. You also face an additional suspension (one year for a first offence; two years for a subsequent offence) under the HTA and up to two years in prison and three years licence suspension under the Criminal Code.

Driving while prohibited

This is a prohibition order under the Criminal Code conviction. When convicted of a violation of the order, you will get a suspension of one year for a first offence or two years for a

subsequent offence. Courts can order longer prohibition, which will be matched in length by a suspension under the Highway Traffic Act.

Note: Suspended drivers must pay $150 to have their licence reinstated. This fee does not apply to reinstatement following a medical or administrative suspension of your driver's licence.

Vehicle Impoundment Program

If you are caught driving while your licence is suspended for a Criminal Code offence, the vehicle you are driving will be impounded for a minimum of 45 days. This applies whether the vehicle is borrowed from a friend or family member, used for business or employment purposes, rented or leased. The owner of the vehicle must pay the towing and storage costs before the vehicle will be released. This program applies to all motor vehicles including passenger vehicles, motorcycles, trucks and buses.

The Vehicle Impoundment Program makes vehicle owners responsible for ensuring that anyone driving their vehicles is not suspended for a Criminal Code conviction. People loaning or renting their vehicles can verify that a driver's licence is valid by phone at 1-900-565-6555 or online at www.mto.gov.on.ca. You can also get a driver's abstract at Driver and Vehicle Licence Issuing Offices or ServiceOntario Kiosks. There is a nominal fee for each licence checked.

Impaired driving

Impaired driving, which means driving when your ability is affected by alcohol or drugs, is a crime in Canada. Your vehicle does not even have to be moving; you can be charged if you are impaired behind the wheel, even if you have not started to drive.

Alcohol

Drinking and driving is a deadly combination.

All drivers must be able to concentrate on driving. Even one drink can reduce your ability to concentrate and react to things that happen suddenly when you are driving. With more alcohol in your blood, you could have trouble judging distances and your vision may become blurred. Factors like tiredness, your mood and how long ago you ate and how much, can make a difference in how alcohol affects your driving ability.

The police have the right to stop any driver they suspect is impaired. They may also do roadside spot checks. When you are stopped by the police, you may be told to blow into a machine that tests your breath for alcohol — a roadside screening device. If you refuse, you will be charged under the Criminal Code. The police will also notify the Registrar of Motor Vehicles and your licence will be suspended immediately for 90 days.

If the reading on the machine shows you have been drinking, you may be taken to a police station for a breathalyser test. The breathalyser uses your breath to measure the amount of alcohol in your bloodstream.

If you cannot give a breath sample for some reason, the police officer can ask you to let a doctor take a blood sample instead. If you are injured and cannot give your consent, a justice of the peace may authorize a doctor to take a blood sample.

The maximum legal blood alcohol concentration for fully licenced drivers is 80 milligrams in 100 millilitres of blood (.08). Any more than .08 is against the law.

If your blood alcohol concentration is more than 80 milligrams in 100 millilitres of blood (.08), you will be charged under the Criminal Code. The police will also notify the Registrar of Motor Vehicles and your licence will be suspended immediately for 90 days. Even if your blood alcohol concentration is less than .08, you can still be charged with impaired driving under the Criminal Code.

If you register in the warn range of .05 to .08 on a roadside screening device, you will receive an **immediate** driver's licence suspension at the roadside. For a first occurrence, you will be suspended for 3 days. For a second occurrence in a five-year period, you will be immediately suspended for 7 days and you must undergo a remedial alcohol education program. For a third or subsequent time in a five-year period, you will be immediately suspended for 30 days and you must undergo a remedial alcohol treatment program and have an ignition interlock condition placed on your licence for 6 months. If you choose not to install an ignition interlock device, you must not drive until the condition is removed from your licence. Meanwhile, if there is no one else available to drive and no safe place to park your vehicle, it will be towed at your expense.

Drugs

Any drug that changes your mood or the way you see and feel about the world around you will affect the way you drive. Criminal Code and HTA suspensions apply to drivers impaired by alcohol or drugs.

Illegal drugs such as marijuana and cocaine are not the only problem. Some drugs that your doctor may prescribe for you and some over-the-counter drugs can also impair your driving. Here are some points you should remember:

- If you use prescription medicines or get allergy shots, ask your doctor about side effects such as dizziness, blurred vision, nausea or drowsiness that could affect your driving.
- Read the information on the package of any over-the-counter medicine you take. Any stimulant, diet pill, tranquillizer or sedative may affect your driving. Even allergy and cold remedies may have ingredients that could affect your driving.
- Drugs and alcohol together can have dangerous effects, even several days after you have taken the drug. Do not take a chance — ask your doctor or pharmacist.

Consider the consequences of impaired driving

Ontario leads the way in combating drinking and driving through some of the toughest laws and programs in North America, including licence suspensions, heavy fines, vehicle impoundment, mandatory alcohol education and treatment programs and the ignition interlock program. Depending on your number of prior convictions, you may be fined up to $50,000, serve time in jail or lose your licence permanently.

For impaired driving that causes injury or death, the penalties are even more severe. If you are convicted of impaired driving causing bodily harm, you may be sentenced to up to 14 years in prison. Impaired driving causing death can carry a sentence of imprisonment for life.

If you drink and drive and are involved in a collision, you may suffer serious injury or cause serious injury to someone else. Your insurance company might not pay for your medical or rehabilitation costs, or for the damage to your or the other person's vehicle and your insurance costs may rise significantly. You may have to pay substantial legal costs as well.

If you are required to drive on the job, a licence suspension could mean losing your job.

Mandatory alcohol education and treatment

If you are convicted of an impaired driving-related Criminal Code offence, you must complete an alcohol education and treatment program during your licence suspension, also referred to as a remedial measures program.

If you are convicted of a drinking and driving related Criminal Code offence, you must take the impaired driving program called *Back on Track*, delivered by the Centre for Addiction and Mental Health. The three-part program, which is available across the province, involves assessment, education or treatment, and follow-up. You must pay for the program. If you have not completed the *Back on Track* program by the time your Criminal Code suspension expires, your licence will be further suspended until you have completed the remedial requirements.

This program also applies to Ontario residents convicted of driving-related Criminal Code offences in any other province of Canada, or equivalent offences in the states of Michigan and New York, as well as to out-of-province drivers who are convicted in Ontario.

If your driver's licence has been suspended for driving in the warn range of .05 to .08 for a second time in a five-year period you must complete a remedial alcohol education program in 120 days from the date of the suspension. For a third or subsequent occurrence of driving in the warn range, you must complete a remedial alcohol treatment program within 180 days from the date of the suspension. You must pay for these remedial programs which are also delivered by the Centre for Addiction and Mental Health. Failure to complete the required remedial program within the specified time period will result in a licence suspension until the remedial program is completed.

Driver improvement interview

The other remedial measures program is for drivers convicted of non-drinking and driving related Criminal Code offences who have no previous alcohol-related convictions. You must undergo a Ministry of Transportation driver improvement interview.

If you have not completed the driver improvement interview

by the time your Criminal Code suspension expires, your licence will be further suspended until you have completed the remedial requirements.

This program also applies to Ontario residents convicted of driving-related Criminal Code offences in any other province of Canada, or equivalent offences in the states of Michigan and New York, as well as to out-of-province drivers who are convicted in Ontario.

Ignition Interlock

An ignition interlock device is an in-car breath screening device. It prevents a vehicle from starting if it detects a blood alcohol concentration over a pre-set limit of 20 milligrams of alcohol per 100 millilitres of blood (.02).

If you are convicted of impaired driving under the Criminal Code of Canada, you are subject to Ontario's Ignition Interlock Program. After serving a licence suspension, completing a mandatory remedial measures program and meeting all licensing conditions, you will be eligible to have your driver's licence back. At that time, an ignition interlock condition is placed on your Ontario driver's licence, which means that you must install an ignition interlock device in your vehicle.

If you choose not to install a device, you must not drive until the condition is removed from your licence. If you are required to complete a road test while the ignition interlock condition is on your licence, you must complete a road test in a vehicle equipped with the device.

You must apply to the Ministry of Transportation to have the condition removed from your licence. If you have completed the minimum period (one year or three years) without any program violations (tampering/driving without/missed appointment with service provider), the ignition interlock condition will be removed. If you do not apply for removal of the licence condition, it will remain on your licence indefinitely.

If your driver's licence has been suspended for driving in the warn range of .05 to .08 for a third or subsequent time in a five-year period, you will also have an ignition interlock condition placed on your licence for 6 months. However, you do not need to apply to the Ministry of Transportation to have the condition removed from your licence. If you have completed the minimum 6-month period without any program violations (tampering/driving

without/missed appointment with service provider), the ignition interlock condition will be removed.

As a vehicle owner, you must not allow a person with an ignition interlock condition to drive your vehicle or you could be convicted of an offence under the Highway Traffic Act. You can find out if a driver has an ignition interlock condition on his or her licence by accessing MTO's website at mto.gov.on.ca or by calling 1-900-565-6555. There is a fee for each licence check.

Chapter 6 — Summary

By the end of this section you should know:

- Your responsibility to maintain a valid driver's licence with the most correct and up to date information
- How the Demerit Point System works for new and fully licensed drivers
- The driving offences that result in a loss of points upon conviction
- Common circumstances where your licence can be cancelled or suspended
- The consequences that can result from a suspended licence including reinstatement fees, remedial measures, ignition interlock, vehicle impoundment and jail time
- How alcohol and drugs impact your ability to drive

Chapter 7

I. Ontario's Drive Clean program

Vehicles powered by gasoline and diesel give off air pollutants and gases such as oxides of carbon, nitrogen and sulphur, hydrocarbons and soot. These pollutants affect the quality of the air we breathe, our health, crop yields and even the global climate.

Hydrocarbons and oxides of nitrogen react in sunlight to form ground level ozone, better known as smog. Smog is a major health hazard responsible for respiratory ailments and other illnesses.

Oxides of sulphur and nitrogen combine with water vapour to form acid rain, which damages our lakes, forests and crops.

Global warming is the result of too much carbon dioxide and other gases trapping heat in our atmosphere. Global warming could cause average temperatures to rise, causing droughts, crop failures, lower water levels and more frequent and severe storms.

Vehicles are the single largest domestic source of smog-causing emissions in Ontario. Drive Clean, administered by the Ministry of the Environment, reduces smog-causing pollutants by identifying grossly polluting vehicles and requiring them to be repaired.

If you own a light-duty vehicle in the Drive Clean Program area (Southern Ontario from Windsor to Ottawa) that is five years old or older and is a 1988 or newer model, you must take your vehicle for a Drive Clean test every two years in order to renew its registration. Light Duty Vehicles manufactured before the 1988 model year are exempt from Drive Clean emissions test

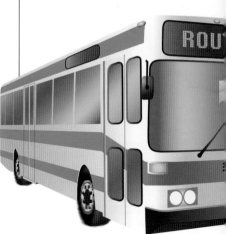

requirements. If you are buying a used vehicle that is older than the current model year and is a 1988 or newer model, the vehicle must pass a Drive Clean test to transfer the ownership and plate it for the road.

Ontario requires all diesel-powered heavy-duty trucks and buses province-wide to pass an annual Drive Clean emissions test. All non-diesel heavy-duty vehicles require annual tests if they are registered in the designated Drive Clean light-duty vehicle program area.

You don't have to wait for a Drive Clean test to do something positive for the environment. Keeping your vehicle well maintained according to the manufacturer's recommended service schedules is an important part of driving clean. For example, if the 'check engine' or 'service engine' lights come on, have your engine looked at by a qualified repair technician as soon as possible. Otherwise, you could face costly repairs to the vehicle's engine or emissions control system.

Please note that the act of creating, distributing or using false Drive Clean passes is an offence under the Environmental Protection Act. Emissions inspectors who do so can be decertified; vehicle owners will be charged.

For more information on Ontario's Drive Clean program, visit www.driveclean.com or call the Drive Clean Call Centre toll-free at 1-888-758-2999.

II. High Occupancy Vehicle (HOV) Lanes

A High Occupancy Vehicle (HOV) lane is a specially designed lane that is designated for use by certain types of vehicles with a specified number of occupants. It can offer travel time savings to those who choose to carpool or take transit. HOV lanes can move a greater number of people than a general traffic lane, and encourage carpooling and transit use by providing travel time savings and a more reliable trip time. HOV lanes are open 24 hours a day, 7 days a week.

HOV lanes benefit all drivers, not only those who carpool, in the following ways:

- Improves highway infrastructure by moving more people in fewer cars
- Reduces the number of vehicles on the road
- Reduces vehicle emissions and improves air quality
- Helps you conserve fuel, save money (by sharing the cost of driving) and reduce stress

HOV lanes on provincial highways are reserved for vehicles carrying at least two people (i.e. a driver plus at least one passenger in any of the following passenger vehicles: cars, minivans, motorcycles, pickup trucks, taxis, buses and limousines).

The HOV lane is separated from the other general traffic lanes by a striped buffer zone. It is illegal and unsafe to cross the striped buffer pavement markings.

Certain vehicles are exempt from the HOV lane rules. Buses can use an HOV lane at any time, regardless of the number of occupants. Emergency vehicles such as police, fire and ambulance are also exempt from the restrictions.

If you use the HOV lanes improperly, you can be stopped and ticketed by a police officer. You will be required to re-enter the general lanes at the next entry/exit zone.

III. Driving efficiently

Vehicles powered by gasoline and diesel give off air pollutants and gases such as oxides of carbon, nitrogen and sulphur, hydrocarbons and soot. These pollutants affect the quality of the air we breathe, our health, crop yields and even the global climate.

Hydrocarbons and oxides of nitrogen react in sunlight to form ground level ozone, better known as smog. Smog is a major health hazard responsible for respiratory ailments and other illnesses. Oxides of sulphur and nitrogen combine with water vapour to form acid rain, which damages our lakes, forests and crops.

A car gives off less carbon dioxide than a larger vehicle, such as an airplane, truck, bus or train, does. However, because so many people own cars and drive them so often, cars are responsible for nearly half the carbon dioxide produced by all forms of transportation. Vehicles that carry large numbers of passengers, such as buses, produce less carbon dioxide per passenger than cars.

As a driver, you can help to protect the environment from the harmful effects of driving by following these suggestions. Many of them can also save you money.

Before you drive:

- Plan ahead. Combine several errands into one trip.
- Avoid driving during rush hours. Driving in off-peak times takes less time, uses less fuel and releases fewer emissions.
- Pay attention to Smog Alerts. It is especially important to follow these suggestions on days when smog is bad.
- For short trips, consider walking or cycling.
- For longer trips, public transit is an environmentally friendly alternative to driving alone.

- Carpool whenever possible. If you want to meet at a central location, there are free carpool lots in many parts of the province. To find one near you, call MTO INFO (416) 235-4686 (1-800-268-4686) or check the MTO website at www.mto.gov.on.ca.

While driving:

- Avoid starting your vehicle unnecessarily. A large burst of pollutants is emitted when a cold engine is started.
- Turn off your vehicle if parked more than 10 seconds. Even in cold weather, vehicle engines warm up within 30 seconds.
- Obey the speed limits. Driving at high speed uses more fuel and increases your chances of a serious collision.
- On the freeway, use your vehicle's overdrive gear and cruise control for better fuel efficiency.
- Remove unnecessary weight

from your vehicle, such as heavy baggage, wet snow and winter sand or salt.
- Maintain your vehicle's aerodynamics. Remove roof racks and compartments when not in use. At high speeds, use your vents instead of opening the windows.
- Use your vehicle's air conditioning wisely. Use your windows and vents in city and stop-and-go traffic. At high speeds, using your air conditioning is usually more fuel efficient than opening your windows and reducing the vehicle's aerodynamics.
- Don't 'top-off' the tank when refueling. Spilled fuel releases harmful vapours.

At the garage:

- Regular maintenance will keep your vehicle running at maximum efficiency, reducing the fuel you need to buy and the pollutants your vehicle emits.

- Keep your vehicle's engine well tuned. Worn spark plugs, dragging brakes, low transmission fluid or a transmission not going into high gear can increase fuel consumption substantially.
- Follow the recommended maintenance schedule in your vehicle owner's manual to maximize fuel efficiency.
- Have any fluid leaks checked by a specialist to avoid engine damage and harming the environment.
- Keep your tires properly inflated to reduce your fuel bill, emissions and tire wear.
- Have your vehicle's alignment checked regularly to reduce uneven tire wear and fuel consumption.

Fuel saving techniques:
Before the trip:

- Inflate tires to the maximum air pressure recommended by the tire manufacturer.

- Carefully fill fuel tanks; do not over-fill; tighten the cap carefully. Allow room for fuel expansion in hot weather.
- Check the engine oil level; do not over-fill.

Starting up:

- Reduce cranking time. A well-tuned engine should start within 30 seconds. Wait two minutes before recranking if it doesn't start the first time.
- Avoid pumping the accelerator (gasoline engines).
- Use the choke correctly (gasoline engines).
- Use the cold weather starting aids correctly. Don't use them to excess.
- Reduce warm-up idling time after starting.

Moving out:

- Do daily trip inspection before starting a gasoline engine and after starting a diesel engine.

- Move out soon and slowly.
- Drive at low speeds initially. Cold engines have high internal friction until they warm up. High speed driving on a cold engine causes excessive wear and unnecessary fuel consumption.
- Increase speed only when the engine is warm.

During the trip:

- Low engine RPM saves fuel, so use progressive shifting.
- Manage your road speed. At highway speeds, the faster you go, the more fuel you will use with any type of bus on any route.
- Whenever possible run in the 70-90 km/h fuel-efficient range. Faster or slower than that, consumption will suffer.
- Match gear to speed. You should always be in a gear where your RPM is as low as possible, at least 200-300 RPM below the governed maximum. You cannot

get good fuel consumption unless you combine efficient engine speed with efficient road speed.

- Minimize idling by shutting down the engine whenever possible, except in very cold weather. Fuel for comfort is a poor investment.
- Maintain a steady cruise speed, the lowest steady speed that will permit on-time arrival at your destination.
- When approaching an upgrade, open the throttle smoothly and shift down only when engine speed makes it necessary.

Operating in traffic:

- Anticipate how traffic conditions are changing and what other drivers will do. By looking ahead, behind and to the sides, maintain an efficient speed or make smaller speed adjustments.
- Select lanes with the smoothest traffic flow.
- Select lanes for efficient speed.

- Maintain a space buffer between your bus and vehicles ahead. This will minimize speed changes and braking. Letting your buffer shrink and expand will make your driving smoother and therefore more fuel efficient. The buffer will also enable you to make safe lane changes without slowing down.

Fuel consumption techniques summary:

If you learn and practise the following techniques, you'll be well on the way to good fuel consumption:

- Use good starting procedures.
- Get going as soon as you can.
- Control your idling.
- Be an RPM miser.
- Use progressive shifting.
- Maintain efficient engine speed.
- Manage your road speed.
- Operate efficiently in traffic.

IV. Mandatory Vehicle Branding program

Under the Mandatory Vehicle Branding program, insurers, self-insurers (fleet owners), auctioneers, importers, salvagers and anyone who deals in used vehicles, are required to determine whether severely damaged and written off ('total loss') vehicles they insure or obtain should be branded either 'Irreparable' or 'Salvage'. They must notify the ministry of the brand through a Notification of Vehicle Brand form. The ministry applies the brand to the vehicle's registration information so that it will appear on the vehicle permit, vehicle abstracts and the Used Vehicle Information Package (UVIP) for that vehicle. The brand identifies the condition of the vehicle to potential buyers. This is how the program helps to protect consumers buying used vehicles.

If your vehicle sustains severe damage and is written off by your insurance company, your insurance company must notify you and the ministry of the brand requirement. If you do not receive a claim settlement through an insurance company, you must have the brand determined by an authorized mechanic at a Type 6 Motor Vehicle Inspection Station. The ministry website has a list of these facilities — visit mto.gov.on.ca for details.

There are four brands:

- A vehicle which has never had a brand applied in Ontario automatically has the brand 'None' applied to its registration documents. However, this does not mean that the vehicle has never been damaged in a collision, was never branded in another jurisdiction or was not rebuilt prior to the mandatory branding program.
- The brand 'Irreparable' means that damage to the vehicle was so severe that the vehicle can be used for parts or scrap only. It cannot

be rebuilt, and it can never be driven in Ontario.

- The brand 'Salvage' means that the damaged vehicle can be repaired or rebuilt. It cannot be registered as fit to drive in Ontario. Once the vehicle has been repaired or rebuilt, and if it can pass a structural inspection to ministry standards, the owner can obtain a Structural Inspection Certificate and have the vehicle branded as 'Rebuilt'.
- The brand 'Rebuilt' means that the vehicle has been previously branded as 'Salvage', but has been rebuilt and has passed a structural inspection to ministry standards. If the vehicle can pass a safety inspection (Safety Standards Certificate), the owner can have it registered as fit to drive in Ontario.

Motorcycles that have been written off must be branded 'Irreparable'; they cannot be branded 'Salvage'.

Trailers, traction engines, farm tractors, mopeds, motorized snow vehicles, street cars or motor vehicles with a model year of 1980 or earlier are exempt from the mandatory branding program.

V. Highway Traffic Act — law relating to school buses

Section 174. (2)
School buses required to stop at railway crossings

The driver of a school bus, within the meaning of section 175, upon approaching on a highway a railway crossing, whether or not it is protected by gates or railway crossing signal lights, unless otherwise directed by a flagman, shall,

a) stop the school bus not less than 5 metres from the nearest rail of the railway;

b) look in both directions along the railway track;

c) open a door of the school bus and listen to determine if any train is approaching;

d) when it is safe to do so, cross the railway track in a gear that will not need to be changed while crossing the track; and

e) not change gears while crossing the railway track.

Section 175. (1)
Definitions

1. In this section, "children" means:
   a) Persons under the age of eighteen, and
   b) In the case where a school bus is being operated by or under a contract with a school board or other authority in charge of a school for the transportation of children to or from school includes students of the school;
   "developmental disability" means a condition of mental impairment, present or occurring during a person's formative years, that is associated with limitations in adaptive behavior,
   "school" does not include a post-secondary school educational institution,
   "school bus" means a bus that:

a) is painted chrome yellow, and
   b) displays on the front and rear thereof the words "school bus" and on the rear thereof the words "do not pass when signals flashing".

2. For the purposes of subsection (3), a motor vehicle shall be deemed to be a bus if it is or has been operated under the authority of a permit for which a bus registration or validation fee was paid in any jurisdiction.

3. No bus, except a bus that at any time during its current validation period is used to transport children or to transport adults who have developmental disabilities, shall be painted chrome yellow.

4. No motor vehicle on a highway, other than a school bus, shall have displayed thereon the words "school bus" or the words "do not pass when signals flashing"

or be equipped with a school bus stop arm.

5. No person shall drive or operate a motor vehicle on a highway that contravenes subsection (3) or (4).

6. Subject to subsection (9), every school bus driver:
   a) Who is about to stop on a highway for the purpose of receiving or discharging children or receiving or discharging adults who have developmental disabilities, shall actuate the overhead red signal-lights on the bus.
   b) As soon as the bus is stopped for a purpose set out in clause (a), shall actuate the school bus stop arm; and
   c) While the bus is stopped for a purpose set out in clause (a) on a highway, shall continue to operate the overhead red signal-lights and stop arm until all passengers having to cross the highway have completed the crossing.

7. Clause 170 (1) (a) does not apply to a driver who stops in accordance with subsection (6).

8. No person shall actuate the overhead red signal-lights or the stop arm on a school bus on a highway under any circumstances other than those set out in subsection (6).

9. No person shall actuate the overhead red signal-lights or the stop arm on a school bus:

a) at an intersection controlled by an operating traffic control signal system;

b) at any other location controlled by an operating traffic control signal system at:

(i) a sign or roadway marking indicating where the stop is to be made;

(ii) the area immediately before entering the nearest crosswalk, if there is no sign or marking indicating where the stop is to be made; or

(iii) a point not less than five metres before the nearest traffic control signal, if there is no sign, marking or crosswalk; or

c) within sixty metres from a location referred to in clause (a) or (b).

10. No person shall stop a school bus on a highway for the purpose of receiving or discharging children or receiving or discharging adults who have developmental disabilities;

a) opposite a designated school bus loading zone; or

b) at a designated school bus loading zone, except as close as practicable to the right curb or edge of the roadway.

11. Every driver or street car operator, when meeting on a highway, other than a highway with a median strip, a stopped school bus that has its overhead red signal-lights flashing, shall stop before reaching the bus and shall not proceed until the bus moves or the overhead red signal-lights have stopped flashing.

12. Every driver or street car operator on a highway, when approaching from the rear a stopped school bus that has its overhead red signal-lights flashing, shall stop at least twenty metres before reaching the bus and shall not proceed until the bus moves or the overhead red signal-lights have stopped flashing.

13. A council of a municipality may, by bylaw, designate school bus loading zones in accordance with the regulations, on highways under its jurisdiction and, where it does so, subsection (6) does not apply to a driver about to stop or stopping in a zone so designated.

14. No by-law passed under subsection (13) becomes effective until the highways or portions thereof affected have signs erected in compliance with this Act and the regulations.

15. The Lieutenant Governor in Council may make regulations:

a) respecting the operation of vehicles used for transporting children or for transporting adults who have developmental disabilities;

b) prescribing the type, design and colour of vehicles referred to in clause (a) and the markings to be displayed thereon;

c) requiring the use of any equipment on or in vehicles referred to in clause (a) and prescribing the standards and specifications of such equipment;

d) prescribing the qualifications of drivers of vehicles referred to in clause (a) and prohibiting the operation thereof by unqualified persons;

e) requiring the inspection of vehicles referred to in clause (a);

f) respecting the designation of school bus loading zones, the location thereof, the erection of signs and the placing of markings on highways;

g) prescribing the books and records that shall be kept by persons who operate vehicles used for transporting children or for transporting adults who have developmental disabilities;

h) requiring the retention of prescribed books and records within vehicles and prescribing the information to be contained and the entries to be recorded in the books or records;

i) governing the service of offence notices for the purposes of subsections (26), (27) and (28), including deeming service to have been effected on a date determined in accordance with the regulations.

16. Any regulation made under subsection (15) may be general or particular in its application.

17. Every person who contravenes subsection (11) or (12) is guilty of an offence and on conviction is liable:

a) for a first offence, to a fine of not less than $400.00 and not more than $2,000.00; and

b) for each subsequent offence, to a fine of not less than $1,000.00 and not more than $4,000.00 or to imprisonment for a term of not more than six months, or to both.

18. An offence referred to in subsection (17) committed more than five years after a previous conviction for either of the offences referred to in subsection (17) is not a subsequent offence for the purpose of clause (17) (b).

19. A person who issues a certificate of offence or who prepares an information to be laid under the *Provincial Offences Act* for a contravention of subsection (11) shall, despite that Act and the regulations under that Act, specify this subsection, instead of subsection (11), as the provision that was contravened, if the defendant is being charged as the owner of the vehicle.

20. A person who issues a certificate of offence or who prepares an information to be laid under the *Provincial Offences Act* for a contravention of subsection (12) shall, despite that Act and the regulations under that Act, specify this subsection, instead of subsection (12), as the provision that was contravened, if the defendant is being charged as the owner of the vehicle.

21. A certificate of offence, offence notice, information or summons that specifies subsection (19) or (20) as the provision that was contravened shall be deemed to specify that subsection (11) or (12) was contravened, as the case may be.

22. No charge shall be dismissed, and no certificate of offence or information shall be quashed, on the basis that a certificate of offence, offence notice, information or summons specifies subsection (19) or (20) instead of subsection (11) or (12) as the provision that was contravened.

23. A certificate of offence or information that specifies subsection (11) or (12) as the provision that was contravened shall not be amended to specify subsection (19) or (20) and a certificate of offence or information that specifies subsection (19) or (20) as the provision that was contravened shall not be amended to specify subsection (11) or (12), without the consent of the prosecutor and the defendant.

24. The purpose of subsections (19) to (23) is to facilitate the use of computer systems that are maintained by the Government of Ontario for recording and processing information related to provincial offences.

25. No summons shall be issued under clause 3 (2) (b) of the *Provincial Offences Act* in proceedings alleging an offence under subsection (19) or (20).

26. An offence notice issued in proceedings alleging an offence under subsection (19) or (20) may be served in accordance with the regulations, in which case subsections 3 (3) to (7) of the *Provincial Offences Act* do not apply.

27. If the provincial offences officer who issues the certificate of offence also serves the offence notice, that officer shall certify, on the certificate of offence, the fact that he or she took the steps authorized by the regulations to serve the offence notice and the date those steps were taken.

28. A certificate referred to in subsection (27) purporting to be signed by the provincial offences officer who issued it shall be received in evidence and is proof of service in the absence of evidence to the contrary.

Regulation 612

1.-(1) Every school bus, as defined in subsection 175 (1) of the Act, shall,

a) display the words "school bus" on the front and rear thereof placed as near as is practicable to the top of the vehicle in a clearly visible position in black letters at least 200 millimetres high with the lines forming the letters being at least 32 millimetres wide on a yellow background;

b) display the words "do not pass when signals flashing" on the rear thereof placed below and as near as is practicable to the words "school bus" in a clearly visible position in black letters not less than 75 and not more than 125 millimetres high with the lines forming the letters having a width

of not less than one-sixth of the height of the letters on a yellow background;

c) be equipped with signal lights that have an effective illuminating area of at least 120 square centimetres, that produce a light of an intensity that is clearly visible at a distance of at least 150 metres and that are attached and operated as follows:

(1) One or two signal lights shall be placed on each side of the front of the bus in as high a position as is practicable and only one light on each side shall operate at a time so as to produce flashes of red light alternately on opposite sides of the bus that are visible only from the front of the bus.

(2) One or two signal lights shall be placed on each side of the rear of the bus in as high a position as is practicable and

as far apart as is practicable and only one light on each side shall operate at a time so as to produce flashes of red light alternately on opposite sides of the bus that are visible only from the rear of the bus.

(3) In the case of a school bus equipped with two signal lights on each side, the two innermost signal lights shall be actuated when the school bus is about to stop on a highway for a purpose described in clause 175 (6) (a) of the Act and the two outermost signal lights shall be actuated while the school bus is stopped on a highway as described in clause 175 (6) (c) of the Act.

(4) The signal lights shall be actuated by a control device accessible to the driver and equipped to give the driver a clear and unmistakable signal either visible or audible when the signal lights are operating;

d) be equipped with a first aid kit,

(i) in the case of a school bus manufactured in accordance with Canadian Standards Association Standard D250-98 or D250-03, that complies with the Standard to which it was manufactured, or

(ii) in the case of a school bus not manufactured in accordance with Canadian Standards Association Standard D250-98 or D250-03, that, unless it complies with either Standard, consists of a sturdy dustproof metal or plastic container containing,

A) four packets each containing four hand cleansers and 12 gauze cleansing pads,

B) 150 individually wrapped 25 millimetre by 75 millimetre adhesive dressings,

C) eight 50 millimetre compress dressings,

D) six 100 millimetre compress dressings,

E) two eye dressing kits each containing one eye shield and two gauze pads,

F) three four-ply gauze dressings at least 900 millimetres square,

G) two 50 millimetre by 5.5 metre gauze bandages,

H) one packet of 25 millimetre by 4.6 metre adhesive tape,

I) six triangular bandages,

J) one 70 millimetre by 610 millimetre rolled metal splint,

K) one pair of scissors,

L) one pair of sliver tweezers, and

M) twelve 50 millimetre safety pins;

e) be equipped with an interior mirror designed and adjusted to provide the seated driver with a view of the passengers, and,

(i) in the case of a school bus manufactured on or after November 30, 1997, comply with Canada Motor Vehicle Safety Standard 111 as it read when the school bus was manufactured, including being equipped with,

A) two rear-view exterior mirrors on each side of the bus, one flat and one convex, and

B) two convex cross-view exterior mirrors consisting of one mirror on each front corner of the school bus, or

ii) in the case of a school bus manufactured before November 30, 1997, having a seating capacity for 24 or more passengers, be equipped with,

A) a convex cross-over exterior mirror, at least 190 millimetres in diameter, securely mounted and adjusted so that the seated driver may see the reflection of the area immediately in front of the front bumper of the bus,

B) a convex right front side-view exterior mirror, securely mounted and adjusted on the roof, right windshield corner post or exterior right rear-view mirror so that the seated driver may observe the reflection of the ground surface immediately adjacent to the right front wheel of the bus, and

C) exterior mirrors securely mounted and adjusted on each side of the vehicle in such a position to afford the seated driver a clearly reflected view of the road-way in the rear and of any vehicle approaching from the rear;

f) in the case of a school bus manufactured on or after the 1st day of September, 1975, having a seating capacity for twenty-four or more passengers, have,

(i) the chassis and the front bumper painted black, and

(ii) the hood, grill and outside surfaces that are in direct line with the seated driver's vision painted lustreless black; and

g) in the case of a school bus manufactured on or after the 1st day of December, 1982, have,

i) the chassis and the front bumper painted black, and

ii) the hood, grill and outside surfaces that are in direct line with the seated driver's vision painted lustreless black.

1.-(1.1) Every school bus referred to in subsection (1) and registered in Ontario shall display,

a) a sign affixed to the bottom of the left window on the rear of the school bus that has the dimensions and bears the markings as illustrated in Figure 1; and

b) a sign affixed to the bottom of the right window on the rear of the bus that has the dimensions and bears the markings as illustrated in Figure 2.

Figure 1

Figure 2

1.-(1.2) If the dimensions of the left or right window on the rear of a school bus cannot accommodate either or both of the signs as required by subsection (1.1), both signs shall be affixed to the rear bumper directly below the locations prescribed by clauses (1.1) (a) and (b).

1.-(1.3) The signs affixed in accordance with subsection (1.1) or (1.2) must be visible at all times to vehicles approaching from the rear of the school bus and shall not be obstructed by any part of or attachment to the school bus.

1.-(1.4) The signs required by subsection (1.1) must meet the performance requirements of any of the types of sheeting specified in the American Society for Testing and Materials Standard D 4956-01a and the sheeting must have a Luminance Factor (Y%) of at least 15.

1.-(2) Every school bus referred to in subsection (1) shall be equipped with a stop arm device that complies with the requirements set out in subsection (3).

1.-(3) A stop arm device shall,

a) be at least 450 millimetres high and 450 millimetres wide and octagonal in shape;

b) display on the front and rear thereof the word "STOP" in white letters at least 150 millimetres high with the lines forming the letters being at least twenty millimetres wide on a red reflectorized background;

c) be equipped with double-faced lamps located in the top and bottom portions of the stop arm, one above the other, that are automatically activated so as to produce alternating flashes of red light, visible to the front and rear of the bus, at the commencement of the stop arm cycle and deactivated when the stop arm is retracted;

d) be installed on the left outside of the bus body and be mounted so as to be readily seen by motorists approaching from the front or rear of the bus when the stop arm is in the extended position;

e) operate automatically so as to move to the fully extended position when the service door of the bus is opened and return to the retracted position when the door is closed; and

f) operate only when the alternating light circuit on the front and rear of the bus is energized.

2.-(1) No person shall operate or permit the operation of a school bus registered in Ontario unless the school bus was manufactured in accordance with,

a) in the case of a school bus manufactured on or after December 1, 1982 and before September 1, 1987, Canadian Standards Association Standard D250-M 1982 or D250-M 1985;

b) in the case of a school bus manufactured on or after September 1, 1987 and before June 1, 2000, Canadian Standards Association

Standard D250-M 1985 or D250-98;

c) in the case of a school bus manufactured on or after June 1, 2000 and before January 1, 2005, Canadian Standards Association Standard D250-98 or D250-03;

d) in the case of a school bus manufactured on or after January 1, 2005, Canadian Standards Association Standard D250-03.

2. No person shall operate or permit the operation of a school bus registered in Ontario and manufactured in accordance with Canadian Standards Association Standard D250-98 or D250-03 unless the school bus continues to meet the Standard to which it was manufactured.

3.-(1) No bus shall be operated by or under contract with a school board or other authority in charge of a school to transport

adults with a developmental disability or children and no bus shall be operated unless,

a) Revoked: O. Reg. 307/00, s. 3.

b) it is equipped with tire chains or snow tires for each driving wheel that is not of the dual type that are placed on the wheels when the conditions of the highway require their use;

c) it is equipped with an accurate speedometer placed to indicate to the driver the speed of the vehicle at all times;

d) it has a body floor constructed and insulated to prevent exhaust gases of the engine from entering the passenger compartment of the vehicle;

e) it is equipped with two windshield wipers that operate at a constant speed and an effective defrosting device that provides clear vision through the windshield and the windows on the left and right sides of the driver;

f) it is equipped with a light or lights arranged to provide light to the whole of the interior except the driver's position, and that are constantly lighted during darkness when there are passengers in the vehicle;

g) it is equipped with an axe or clawbar and an adequate fire extinguisher both securely mounted in such a manner and place as to be readily accessible;

h) it is equipped with dependable tires that in the case of front tires have not been rebuilt;

i) it is equipped with at least one door or exit and,

(i) a door or exit for emergency use situated at the rear of the vehicle or near the rear on the left side of the vehicle and which has a door lock equipped with an interior handle which releases the lock when lifted up, or

(ii) subject to subsection (2), at least three pushout windows on each side of the passenger compartment of the vehicle each of which,

A) has a minimum height of 500 millimetres and a minimum width of 760 millimetres,

B) is designed, constructed and maintained to open outwards when a reasonable amount of manual force is applied to the inside of the window, and

C) displays on or adjacent to the window adequate directions for its emergency use.

3.-(2) A motor vehicle that is equipped in accordance with subclause (1) (i) (ii) shall be equipped with an additional pushout window located in the rear of the vehicle.

6. For the purposes of this Regulation, the date that a school bus was manufactured shall be deemed, in the absence of evidence to the contrary, to be the date on the school bus's compliance label.

Regulation 468

1.(1) An offence notice issued in a proceeding against an owner of a motor vehicle for an offence under subsection 175 (19) or (20) of the Act may be served by regular prepaid mail to the person charged, at the address of the holder of the plate portion of the permit as it appears in the Ministry's records, within 23 days after the occurrence of the alleged offence.

1.(2) Service of an offence notice that has been mailed in accordance with subsection (1) shall be deemed to have been effected on the seventh day after the day it was mailed.

2. If the provincial offences officer who issued the certificate of offence also serves the offence notice on the person charged, that officer shall certify on the certificate of offence the fact that the offence notice was mailed and the date it was mailed.

3. Where an offence notice is served in accordance with this Regulation by a person other than the provincial offences officer who issued the certificate of offence, the person shall complete an affidavit of service.

Chapter 7 — Summary

By the end of this chapter you should know:

- What Ontario's Drive Clean program is and how it works
- What High Occupancy Vehicle (HOV) lanes are and how they work
- Techniques for driving efficiently and saving fuel
- What the Mandatory Vehicle Branding program is and how it works
- Some of the laws that relate to school buses

Conversion chart

Imperial to Metric Converter

From	To	Multiply By
inches	centimetres	2.54
miles	kilometres	1.61
feet	metres	0.31
pounds	kilograms	0.46
miles per hour	kilometres per hour	1.61

Metric to Imperial Converter

From	To	Multiply By
centrimetres	inches	0.39
kilometres	miles	0.62
metres	feet	3.28
kilograms	pounds	2.21
kilometres per hour	miles per hour	0.61

Personalize your licence plates — with two to eight characters, as well as a great choice of colour graphics. Then you'll really stand out from the crowd.

Turn the page to find out more.

NOW THERE ARE MORE WAYS THAN EVER TO EXPRESS YOURSELF!

WE'RE HELPING YOU BUILD CHARACTERS.

Now you've got extra choices when creating your personalized licence plate. We've introduced seven and eight characters. So you've got even more to work with — a minimum of two characters and right up to eight. Just think of the possibilities.

Every personalized plate is one of a kind. No one else can have the same plate as yours.

For more information and to order your personalized plates, call 1-800-AUTO-PL8 (1-800-288-6758).

**Or visit the ServiceOntario website: www.serviceontario.ca
Or drop by your local Driver and Vehicle Licence Issuing Office
Or one of 70 ServiceOntario kiosks.**

Gift certificates are available too.

Graphic licence plates are a hit! And now there are more than 40 choices available. Support your favourite Ontario sports team, community or arts organization, professional group or university. Or select a timeless icon like the loon or trillium.

For a totally unique look, add a colour graphic to a personalized plate with up to six characters.

So express yourself — with colour graphics and personalized licence plates.

For more information and to order your plates, call 1-800-AUTO-PL8 (1-800-288-6758).

Or visit our website: www.mto.gov.on.ca
Or drop by your local Driver and
Vehicle Licence Issuing Office
Or one of 70 ServiceOntario kiosks.

Gift certificates
are available too.

ADD SOME COLOUR WHERE IT COUNTS.

Other MTO Publications for you

Copies of this handbook and others may be purchased from a:

- Retail store near you;
- DriveTest Centre;
- Driver and Vehicle Licence Issuing Office; or
- Publications Ontario

50 Grosvenor Street

Toronto, Ontario

M7A 1N8

- www.publications.serviceontario.ca

or by calling

(416) 326-5300

or 1-800-668-9938 (toll free)

(416) 326-5317 (fax)

Prepayment required by cheque or credit card — VISA or Mastercard. You may also pay with a certified cheque at DriveTest Centres.

Handbook prices are subject to 5% G.S.T. and 5% shipping costs. Please add 10% to your total purchase to cover G.S.T. and shipping cost. Map is subject to 5% G.S.T., 8% P.S.T. and 5% shipping costs. Please add 18% to your total purchase to cover G.S.T. and shipping cost.

The Official Driver's Handbook
$ 14.95
ISBN 978-1-4249-4041-7

The Official Motorcycle Handbook
$ 14.95
ISBN 978-1-4249-4043-1

The Official Truck Handbook
$ 18.95
ISBN 978-1-4249-4045-5

The Official Bus Handbook
$ 18.95
ISBN 978-1-4249-4047-9

The Official Air Brake Handbook
$ 18.95
ISBN 978-1-4249-4049-3

The Official Ontario Road Map
$ 2.95
ISBN 0-7794-4210-5